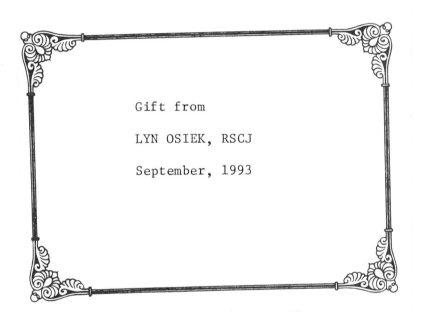

New Visions

NEW VISIONS

Historical and Theological Perspectives on the Jewish-Christian Dialogue

EDITED BY
VAL AMBROSE McINNES, O.P.

A Tulane Judeo-Christian Studies Edition
CROSSROAD • NEW YORK

In memory of
and
in gratitude to

Rabbi Marc H. Tanenbaum
and
Msgr. John M. Oesterreicher

extraordinary visionaries
in the interfaith dialogue

1993
The Crossroad Publishing Company
370 Lexington Avenue, New York, NY 10017

Printed in the United States of America

Library of Congress Cataloging-in-Publication Data

New visions : historical and theological perspectives on the Jewish
-Christian dialogue / edited by Val Ambrose McInnes.
    p. cm. — (A Tulane Judeo-Christian studies edition) (Tulane
Chair of Judeo-Christian Studies series ; v. 3)
    ISBN 0-8245-1246-4
    1. Judaism—Relations—Christianity. 2. Christianity and other
religions—Judaism. 3. Judaism—History—Talmudic period, 10–425.
4. Christianity—Early church, ca. 30–600. 5. Judaism (Christian
theology) 6. Religion—Philosophy. I. McInnes, Val A.
II. Series. III. Series; Tulane Chair of Judeo-Christian Studies
series ; v. 3.
BM535.N39   1993
261.2′6—dc20   93-4190
                                                                        CIP

Contents

Preface

ON DECEMBER 8, 1990, the Roman Catholic Church marked the twenty-fifth anniversary of the closing of the Second Vatican Council. Six years have passed since the extraordinary Synod of Bishops convened by Pope John Paul II to celebrate the twentieth anniversary of the completion of the Council and to assess the state of its implementation. The work of implementing the Council's program of renewal continues throughout the world. It is an important task. Pope John XXIII foresaw that the Council would be the instrument of the Holy Spirit and would renew the Church and the world, "as through a new Pentecost."

The passage of over a quarter of a century since the close of Vatican II provides an opportunity for taking stock of its accomplishments, the "aggiornamento" within the Church and the struggle for unity among the Christian churches and the renewal of the dialogue with our Jewish sisters and brothers in the Lord. At the same time, it provides an opportunity to see the relevance of the Jewish-Christian tradition for the dialogue with the rest of the world religions and of all God's people.

The opportunity of sharing new historical visions presents itself today based on new insights into the Jewish-Christian dialogue. Historically speaking, scholars like Professor Sean Freyne are shedding new light on the origins of the Jewish-Christian encounter from the first to the fourth centuries. He describes how traces of anti-Semitism are presently manifest in the New Testament, and especially in John's Gospel.

Other scholars, like Professor Robert L. Wilken, are pulling the curtain back on aspects of the early model of holiness and virtue common to both Christians and Jews.

A new theological basis for the Jewish-Christian dialogue today and tomorrow is articulated with great sensitivity by Professor Jürgen Moltmann in his significant contribution *Christology in the Christian-Jewish Dialogue*. The very title reveals how the word "dialogue" implies that we live in a relationship with one another. It also implies the possibility of understanding each other and of standing in the place of one another. This willingness to commune intellectually with each other and to expect each religious tradition are the bridges for dialogue.

Rabbi Jakob Petuchowski underscores the continuity in Jewish-Christian worship by revealing the Jewish model within Christ's prayer, the Our Father.

Professor Lawrence E. Frizzell produces a comprehensive study on the Catholic Church and the Jewish people today— evaluating the historical results of the influence of the Second Vatican Council on the Jewish-Christian dialogue in recent years. He reveals the common threads of dialogue and the tremendous strides made in the last twenty-six years. Yet he is quick to point out the unfulfilled and unfinished hopes and expectations of the Jewish-Christian dialogue for today and tomorrow. His focus is on the past twenty-six years as the basis for present and future fulfillment of the dialogue.

Freyne, Wilken, Moltmann, and Frizzell all emphasize the need for Christian theology to revise seriously its vision of relations between Israel and the Church. Christian theology of Judaism has dramatically changed in the last twenty-six years, but it is still in many ways in its infancy.

Recently, Professor Claude Geffré, O.P., suggests three directions in which exegetical and theological research can reorient itself in respect to considering Judaism as a sister religion.*

First he points out the question of discovering the traces of anti-Judaism already manifested in the writings of the New Testament, and in particular the tendency, especially in the Johannine writings, to identify the Chief Priest and the Scribes with the Jewish people as a whole. He emphasizes the need to

---

*Professor Claude Geffré, O.P., "New Trends in French Theology," unpublished paper for the Chair of Judeo-Christian Studies, spring of 1992.

elaborate a new hermeneutic, based upon our historic present and future expectations of the dialogue.

Secondly, he raises the question of the permanent election of the Jewish people, regarded from that time onward as a source of grace for the whole believing community. According to St. Paul's teaching in Romans 9–11, the alliance and the promise made to Israel are irrevocable on God's part. Properly speaking, Professor Geffré emphasizes that the Church is not a new Israel. Nor, contrary to traditional teaching of Christian theology, is the Jewish people as a whole excluded from the source of salvation because of its refusal to believe in Jesus. We have to seek theologically to reconcile the novelty of the Church as the new people of God with the permanence of the promise made to Israel. These are areas where theologians like Rosenzweig have contributed significantly to the dialogue in his *The Star of Redemption*. The complementary role of the Church and the Jewish people has not been fully manifested. This is part of the unfinished business of the dialogue.

Finally, the burning question of Israel's return to its own land as the State of Israel is a sign of the permanence of the divine promise made to the Jewish people. But many scholars do not want to link the Jewish people to the historical identity of the State of Israel. There are a number of scholars, both Jews and Christians, who are beginning to think that the modern State of Israel puts at risk and compromises the special vocation of the Jewish people among the nations of the world. These are a few of the directions in which the Jewish-Christian dialogue needs to develop.

The two concluding chapters provoke our thinking beyond the traditional Judeo-Christian context, from what might be called a "confessional ecumenism" to a "planetary ecumenism," to encompass the global picture of a religious pluralism. Fortunately, since the fall of the Communist empire, the question of belief and unbelief is framed not so much in political ideological terms, but now more accurately in terms of the religious ideologies found in the rich spectrum of Moslem, Hindu, Shintoist, and Buddhist traditions.

Professor John Macquarrie raises the fundamental question of belief or non-belief as found in the philosophy of religion of Heidegger. His analysis of Heidegger's philosophy of religion sets the stage for a discussion of panentheism and not pantheism, which is, as Professor Macquarrie stresses, something entirely different. Heidegger saw the importance of thinking through the question of God in terms of the Event as something beyond being. Here, Macquarrie interprets what he would call the "totally other" mystical reality which tradition calls God. According to Macquarrie, Heidegger forces us to think through Heidegger's notion of Event in the context of his uniquely non-theological inquiry. It is the question behind all questions.

The concluding contribution to this volume is made by the distinguished English Bishop of Durham, David Jenkins. For him, the theological question is no longer the parochial one solely in the context of the Jewish-Christian dialogue. It is the question of monotheism addressed to all of the great religions of the world. The exclusivity of Judaism and Christianity raises the question of the separateness with the other great religions of the world. Where does the future of religion lie in the twenty-first century? What is it that the one God of the universe wants us to do with the whole of the world, and not necessarily from our own human and parochial religious perspectives? In other words, what is the new vision that the Jewish-Christian dialogue gives to the rest of the world, to the one world that God himself has made, and all the people in it?

The central question in the Jewish-Christian dialogue is how do Jews and Christians accept one another's truth without abandoning their own religion, and with it their own identity? Yet perhaps the real question is what is the deeper religious identity at the heart of every person and every religion? This volume, in its diverse ways, is a modest attempt to address that question and to give new visions and directions for the religious dialogue of the twenty-first century.

VAL AMBROSE MCINNES, O.P.

Christians in a Jewish World:
The First Century

SEÁN FREYNE

AS MY TOPIC for these two essays I have chosen to explore the encounter between Jews and Christians in the first and the fourth centuries of the common era. For Christianity, the first century is its founding period, and in the case of the Jews, Jacob Neusner, the distinguished Jewish scholar, has called the fourth century the real first century, for reasons that will emerge in the next essay.[1] These two time periods suggested themselves to me as useful sounding boards for exploring Jewish-Christian relations—both the possibilities and the difficulties—because in the first century the Jews were the dominant force in this particular relationship, whereas in the fourth the Christians had begun to take the upper hand with Constantine's conversion and the gradual Christianization of the empire, east and west. It should be instructive to see how each tradition handled its position of dominance, socially and theologically, while at the same time exploring the ways in which each in turn coped with the position of subordination.

An examination of how such closely related traditions as Judaism and Christianity interacted with each other in their formative periods has an inherent interest of its own. In view of the impact that one of those traditions has had in shaping our western society, and because of the legacy of mutual recriminations that has been handed down to us in our sacred texts, Jewish and Christian, from those centuries, it surely is incumbent on both traditions to re-examine their origins to see if some revision of age-old stereotypes might not be possible.

11

Fortunately, there are encouraging signs in recent scholarship that such a revision is possible, particularly as we become more aware of the ways in which religious traditions are bound up with larger questions of culture and language, being shaped by factors that we would describe as non-religious, and in turn functioning as shaping factors in the social worlds of people.[2] No religious tradition appears in a clear blue sky from a mythical golden age, however much all religions would like to authenticate their claims by suggesting as much. For some there is a dangerous relativism in this kind of discussion. Yet, given the dogmatisms of both traditions, Jewish and Christian, some relativization of the claims by both might not be misplaced.

The Jewish World of Early Christian Experience

Judaism, in the sense of a single religious system, is a modern creation; the historical reality was quite different. The task of scholarship is to introduce differentiation and definition into a field that has for too long been viewed in a highly uncritical manner. Analogous to the way in which some Roman Catholics still think that the Holy Roman Catholic Church, papacy and all, was put securely in place by Jesus before he died, the orthodox Jewish point of view has been that Rabbinic Judaism as we find it in the Mishnah and Talmud was a completed system already from the time of the Babylonian exile onwards. Such ideological readings of history have no feel for change, development, or process; there is no concern with analyzing the factors that make for difference in human affairs. Yet it is these very factors and the way they receive concrete expressions that prove to be the interesting things about history—any history, whether it be first-century C.E. Palestine or nineteenth-century Ireland, to take a local example with which I am somewhat familiar.

The Babylonian exile did indeed have a profound effect on later Jewish self-expression. That experience of exile, so poignantly expressed in Psalm 137—"By the waters of Babylon we sat and wept"—was to remain an ongoing tension for Jews, even to our own time. The loss of the symbol of the land as God's gift and guarantee of covenant fidelity was a profound shock to the Jewish religious *psyche*—at least for those experiencing exile. And for those who remained behind, the loss of their religious center, Jerusalem and its temple, was equally demoralizing. In exile other ways of being Jewish did inevitably emerge—prayer meetings, study houses, and the like. These would become the new centers of restored Judaism after the destruction of the second temple five centuries later.[3] Even contacts with such Eastern religious traditions as Zoroastrianism cannot be discounted. Life goes on and people are extraordinarily resilient in the face of seemingly irresistible forces with which they have to come to terms. When the opportunity to return to the homeland was eventually given through the Persian king Cyrus, the anointed of the Lord (Is. 45:1), many Jews availed of the opportunity, but others chose not to, and found nothing incompatible with their way of being Jewish by taking that option.

Two centuries later the conquests of Alexander the Great and the resulting one-world philosophy that gave theoretical expression to those conquests, was to pose a rather different challenge to Jewish self-understanding. The lure of the cities that emerged everywhere in the Near East, with the inevitable mixing of cultures that took place, was an exciting prospect in itself. Moreover, the Israelite tradition had a strong universalist strain symbolized by the original Patriarch Abraham, the source of universal blessing (Gn. 12:3). This vision had survived intact, despite the exilic experience, mainly through the visionary symbolism of the later prophets and their proto-apocalyptic world-view of a new age. Although it would be difficult to document, given the nature of our sources, it is by no means preposterous to suggest that Jews adapted to the one world of Alexander rather well, not just because of the economic benefits it offered (e.g., 1 Macc. 1:11) but also for religious reasons. True, a book such as *Qoheleth* suggests that the encounter with the Greek *geist* could be corrosive of authentic Jewish faith, but the flowering of wisdom theology in such books as *Proverbs* and the *Wisdom of Solomon* represents a different type of intellectual response to the challenges of the new universalist outlook.[4] Wisdom was not tied to any one ethnic group but was an international phenomenon in the Ancient Near East for millenia. It could be easily wedded to the earlier Israelite creation myths with their sense of the unity of the whole human family. In the same spirit, such early Jewish apologists as Artapanus and Pseudo Hecataeus were striving to show that there was no incompatibility between Jewish faith and Greek reason. It was a line of argument that Christian apologists too would develop and for which they were indebted to their Jewish antecedents.[5]

While Jews of the Diaspora were settling down to life in the cosmopolis, armed with a Greek translation of their sacred writings (the LXX or Septuagint) and enjoying the economic benefits, often with their rights as Jews protected by charter of the hellenistic kings, those in the homeland were about to experience another shock that would leave a deep scar on the Jewish self-understanding. The attempt of Antiochus IV, Epiphanes, to introduce the worship of Zeus in Jerusalem in 167 B.C.E., aided by what the first book of Maccabees calls wicked and lawless men from among us, although short-lived, brought about realignments of Jews in the homeland that were to have lasting significance. The political wing of the resistance, the Maccabees/Hasmoneans, emerged in the first century B.C.E. as a Hellenized but Jewish aristocracy, to the extent that through their wars of conquest, they had developed a Jewish state with a bureaucracy and army that was thoroughly Greek in its professionalism and style. Others, the Hasidim, took the religious concerns of the persecution more seriously, and for them any contacts with the non-Jewish world were threatening and to be avoided. There was need to draw clear boundaries between Jew and non-Jew and indicate where the correct lines could be established. Only thus could order be restored and the threatened chaos averted. Those Jews who would seek to disrupt that order or violate its boundaries were to be treated with suspicion, if not downright hostility. The Wicked Priest and the Man of Lies, opponents of the Teacher of Righteousness, are just two examples of this intra-Palestinian Jewish tension which appear in the writings of the Essene community from Qumran (the Dead Sea Scrolls).[6] On the other side the attitude of Alexander Janaeus, a Hasmonean king of the first century B.C.E. who had eight hundred Pharisees crucified for challenging his rights to the high priesthood, is symptomatic of the deep divisions that were the legacy of Antiochus' reform and the reactions to it.[7]

The divisions were not just religious; they were social also. For those Jews who did not, or could not take the Diaspora option, the so-called "people of the land," ownership of a plot of land with the resulting obligation to bring tithes of what it produced to the central shrine at Jerusalem, gave concrete expression to their pious hopes and aspirations. The increased burden of taxation and the ravages of the Hasmonean wars of conquest, followed by the civil strife of the Herodian and early Roman periods, created serious economic pressure for the Jewish peasant in the homeland. The fact that by the first century C.E. their overlords (often absentee landlords) were Jewish and priestly added a new dimension to the tensions. It is little wonder that in the century in which early Christianity was to emerge from the Palestinian Jesus movement, several other movements of social protest with their leaders adopting a messianic guise were to surface within Palestinian Jewish life.[8] Within this setting of religious divisions, social unrest, regional variations, and competing movements of liberation, we are to, locate the Jesus movement. Each group understood the symbols of temple, torah, and land in the light of their own political and social aspirations, thereby giving rise to what may be described in sociological categories as Jewish sectarianism of the first century.

Apart from the Jesus movement, the only other group to survive the turmoil of the first Jewish revolt against Rome (66–70 C.E.) was the Pharisees. Although estimates of this party's significance vary, modern critical scholarship is at one in seeing the group, with its concerns for a distinctive Jewish identity in terms of dietary and other purity laws, as the nucleus from which the great Rabbinic system of later centuries was to emerge.[9] The period after 70 was indeed a traumatic one for Jews. Their temple was destroyed once again and their political aspirations shattered. If Judaism was to survive, it would have to find another center and redefine itself in relation to that. This was a period of deep soul searching. Shattered hopes for a new age are not the most reliable building blocks of a new religious system. The temptation to abandon the Jewish religious vision entirely was real—the flight to Gnosticism with its vision of this world as essentially evil. It is against this climate of religious doubt and uncertainty that we are to judge the new beginnings that the heirs of Pharisaism brought about, however much their achievement was to mean a hostile encounter with the other option arising from a pre-70 Palestinian Judaism, namely emerging Catholic Christianity. If we are to correctly evaluate early Christianity's encounter, often hostile, with its Jewish world, it is against this background that we must understand it.

Our survey of the Jewish world of early Christians has been highly selective, often general and sketchy.[10] Nonetheless, enough has hopefully been said to break down some prevailing stereotypes, even among some scholars in the field. First-century Judaism emerges as a highly complex phenomenon, the product of various historical social and religious factors that had been operative for several centuries. It is a world of shifting centers and changing significance for old symbols. Temple, torah and land are common to all Jews, but the understanding of each and the resulting social configurations varied considerably. The priest, the sage, and the freedom fighter emerge as different types, giving concrete expression to those different understandings. Yet, like all ideal types, none of these is totally exclusive of the others. It is, rather a question of which strand is dominant in shaping the way in which the others are perceived. At the center of the struggle is the question of how Israel is to be defined, and where God's people, the heir to Abraham's promises, is to be located. It is time now to turn to the question of Christian encounter with this world. We should be better equipped to understand the tensions, the animosities and the rhetoric as well as the agreements.

Christians in a Jewish World—The First Generation

It is commonplace today to emphasize the Jewishness of Jesus and his first followers, but this recognition is not always free of ulterior motives. On the Jewish side, the portrait of Jesus is often a watered-down one—Jesus espoused the heart and soul of Jewish piety; while Christians have tended to use the Jewish background of Jesus to emphasize his religious superiority vis-à-vis his contemporaries, thereby at least implicitly, reflecting later Christological thinking about him based on the resurrection faith.[11] Furthermore, the tensions between the Jesus movement in its Pauline version and various forms of Jewish observance are sometimes attributed to Paul's abandoning of his Jewish faith for Hellenistic syncretism. In this account the tensions between early Christianity and its parent are attributable to Paul's anti-Jewish stance, whereas Jesus is totally exonerated. What is called for is a historically plausible account of the Jewishness of Jesus that also recognizes the fact that he and his movement were rejected by certain elements of Jewish society, namely, the influential priestly aristocracy based in Jerusalem. We cannot here attempt such an account. Suffice it to say that in my view, the fact that Jesus was a Galilean played no small part in his rejection. By calling into question the absolute centrality of Jerusalem and its temple through an itinerant, rural ministry, Jesus had already left himself open to the charge of subverting the symbolic center of Jewish faith—with all the economic and social implications of such a radical position for those who lived off the tithing, pilgrimage, and other bonds that held temple and land together.[12] No self-respecting temple religion could tolerate such a challenge to its own control of the redemptive media. In addition, the refusal to recognize property, land, and family as absolute signs of God's favor called into question the assumptions and values that held that society together. Here at one and the same time was a challenge to the prevailing symbolic system, and an upheaval of the social world that underpinned it, that could not be tolerated.

One of the most difficult aspects of early Christian history to unravel is the question of how and why a movement that was unacceptable to the Jewish religious establishment in the person of its founder came to be viewed rather differently in the person of his brother, James, the head of the Jerusalem Church, according to *Acts of the Apostle*. Of course not all members of the new movement were acceptable in Jerusalem. After Stephen's challenge to temple, torah, and land with his daring proclamation that God's election was not tied to those dwelling in the land, and that God took no pleasure in temples made with hands (i.e., idolatrous ones, Acts 7)—the Hellenists, or Greek-speaking Jewish Christians, were driven from Jerusalem, whereas the Aramaic-speaking Jews who had believed in Jesus were allowed to stay, under James's leadership.[13] It is true that another James, the son of Zebedee, suffered martyrdom in Jerusalem under Herod Agrippa 1, Herod the Great's grandson, a little later (Acts 12:2f), an episode that almost certainly occasioned the transfer of Peter from Jerusalem to Antioch.

It was in Antioch that the new movement had first made a clear break with its Jewish moorings, proclaiming the gospel, not just to God-fearers (i.e., Jewish sympathizers) but to complete pagans. Appropriately, it was there that its members received the new name Christian, a fact that clearly points to the social differentiation that was taking place. Not that that meant an immediate and total break. As late as the year 49 C.E., Suetonius, a Roman historian, tells us that Jews were expelled from Rome because of the disruptions caused by a certain Chrestos. This is generally taken to refer to controversies about Jesus as the Christ among Rome's large Jewish population. Obviously, these disputes were sufficiently acrimonious to be seen by Roman officialdom as disturbing the peace. But the important point from our perspective is the fact that the problem, as seen from the outside, was regarded as a *Jewish* problem.

Meanwhile, Paul, the self-styled "apostle of the gentiles," had been building on the foundations laid by the Hellenists at

Antioch, bringing the gospel about Jesus Christ to the gentiles. In the past, the History of Religions School of New Testament scholarship viewed Paul as being influenced not by his Jewish training and background, but rather by the Greco-Roman religious and philosophical ethos of the Mediterranean world. As mentioned earlier, it was Paul, not Jesus who had sowed the seeds of the ultimate break with Judaism in that view. Recent Pauline scholarship however, has shown how distorted this understanding is.[14] He was, and remained, thoroughly Jewish in his faith, his orientation, and his thinking. Why then the violent opposition to him? In fact although Paul does mention being punished by a Jewish court more than once (2 Cor. 11:24 f.), the main source of his opposition came not from Jewish authorities, but from other members of the new movement of a Pharisaic background, who sought to insist on circumcision for all converts.[15] In other words, Paul's battles are about the correct understanding and application of the universal dimensions of his Jewish faith, which other elements in the Jesus movement also shared, but applied rather differently. Did one have to become a practicing Jew—circumcision, dietary laws, sabbaths, and the rest—to share the blessings of the messianic age that Paul and others believed had finally dawned? Paul's answer was an unequivocal no; gentiles too could share the blessings without becoming observant Jews. Thus, as Wayne Meeks has expressed it, *theologically* speaking the Pauline churches are thoroughly Jewish, but *socially* there seems to have been little enough interaction between Pauline Christians and Jewish congregations in places like Asia Minor or Greece.[16] Once Paul had become the apostle to the gentiles, his contacts with his mother religion were primarily through fellow converts to Jesus, but those who viewed their present situation rather differently from him.

Yet, not even these conservative Jewish Christians at Jerusalem could ultimately cloak the emerging gulf between the new movement and its parent. Perhaps it was the refusal of the Jerusalem Christians to become embroiled in the messianic-style struggle for freedom that was simmering in Jerusalem and

Judea. Or it may have been differences in theological thinking on worship—or a combination of these and other factors. Although later Christian apocryphal tradition represents James as a just man, a *hasid*, who visited the temple daily, even officiating as high priest once, we know that historically he too suffered the same fate as Jesus, and his namesake James, the son of Zebedee, at the hands of the Jewish high priest and Sanhedrin, being stoned to death in 62 C.E., during an interregnum between two Roman procurators of Judea. (Josephus *Ant* 20:200). This was probably the occasion for the flight to Pella of the Jerusalem Christians mentioned by Eusebius (Eccles. Hist. 111,5.3). Some have queried the authenticity of this account. Yet the appearance in the Transjordan region of a number of Jewish Christian groups, like the Ebionites and the Nazoreans, whose views appear to be similar to those of the Jerusalem Christians we hear about in the New Testament, suggests that such a migration did in fact take place.[17] Our knowledge of these Jewish Christians is extremely sketchy, yet their existence bears witness to the fact that a form of Christian self-understanding that was much closer to emerging orthodox Jewish practice than any of those expressed in the New Testament continued to exist well into the second century. Indeed, the interesting suggestion has been made that perhaps it is through these "forgotten Christians" that a very positive memory of Jesus found its way into Islam, when that whole region was overrun in the Muslim conquests of the sixth century.

To sum up the discussion in this section of the paper, we can say that a survey of early Christian self-expressions in relation to the prevailing Jewish world suggests a considerable diversity, corresponding with, and in part related to, the diversity of Jewish experience we encountered earlier. With hindsight we can clearly see a line going from Paul through Stephen back to Jesus that would inevitably mean separation into quite diverse "great traditions," later to be labeled Jewish and Christian. Yet in the period we have examined thus far it is fair to say that we are still dealing with an intra-Jewish debate. As the debate is most clearly articulated in Paul's writings, it has to do with exclusivity of the call to Israel and the access of the Gentiles to salvation. But there are other aspects also detectable in the earliest stratum of our gospels—a prophetic apocalyptic group that continued the lifestyle of Jesus and his criticism of the Jerusalem aristocracy's monopoly of access to God on the one hand, and a Christian Pharisaism that found Pauline libertinism a betrayal of their birthright on the other. We know less about the Diaspora situation apart from the Pauline churches, but men like Barnabas and those anonymous Jews of Cyrene who brought the good news to the Gentiles at Antioch also played an important role in shaping early Christian beliefs and practices (Acts 11:19–26). They must have relied heavily on the style of the Jewish Diaspora communities in its encounter with paganism; they certainly used their Greek Bible to argue their claims. We simply do not have the information to complete the picture, but we can clearly see that the early Christian interaction with its parent religion had many facets and not a few contradictions.

Christians in a Jewish World—The Second Generation

It would be interesting to speculate on how the relationship between the Jesus movement (in its diverse forms) and the other varied forms of Judaism (both Palestinian and Diaspora) might have developed had the trauma of the Jewish War of 66–70 C.E. not changed the perspective for both sides. We have already seen that on the Jewish side a whole new way that would apply to all Jews had to be articulated now that the temple with its elaborate system of pilgrimages and sacrifices had been removed. Of course, the hope of rebuilding must have been real. In the recently published Temple Scroll from Qumran we hear of three different temples—the existing one that is illegitimate and inhabited by the sons of Belial, the interim one the Essenes apparently hoped to build where God would allow his glory to dwell, and the eschatological one that Yahweh himself would build (column 29).[18] There was then precedent for destruction and hope for rebuilding, and as far that hope remained active,

Jacob Neusner is correct in saying that the real shock to Judaism came not with the destruction in 70 but with the failure to rebuild at the time of the Bar Cochba War seventy years later when Hadrian threatened instead to build a temple to the Capitoline Jupiter on the temple mount.[19]

Notwithstanding such hopes, however, arrangements had to be made in the interim, and the group that had centered its life on the home and village, rather than the temple and the holy city (the Pharisees), was best equipped emotionally and theologically to fashion an alternative way. The scribe with the Torah Scroll was eventually to replace both the priest and his altar and the freedom fighter with his emblems of liberation as the repository of Israel's hopes, by articulating God's will in the present. Although the pluralism remained, the social and political balance on which it was based had been disrupted and gradually one strand from the tangled skein of the pre-70 days began to dominate as the sages, the heirs of the Pharisaic scribes of the earlier period, took over as the intellectual and religious leaders of the Jewish faith. It is their views that were to give shape and focus to the emerging Judaism that was eventually to flower with the literary productions of rabbinic Judaism: Mishnah, Tosefta, Palestinian and Babylonian Talmuds, as well as the various Midrashim or interpretative compilations of Scriptural exegesis. At the same time a more popular form of Jewish piety found its expression in the synagogue prayer service, echoes of which are undoubtedly to be heard in the Targumim, or Aramaic paraphrases of the Bible, which were performed in association with the public reading of the Scripture. The question of the extent of the sages' input into and control of the synagogue worship is disputed, yet the probability is that it was considerable.[20] It was with this emerging Jewish orthodoxy, which had its roots in earlier halachic practices associated with the Pharisees, that the developing Christian Church of the second century had to contend.

For all branches of the Christian movement, the fall of the Jerusalem temple raised a different set of questions. As we have suggested already, there was an intrinsic challenge to the temple's symbolic value in Jesus' itinerant ministry, proclaiming God's mighty presence in his own group of fellow travelers.[21] Stephen and the Hellenists had picked up that critique and based their view of mission on the new understanding of God that was inherent in it. Now that the temple was actually destroyed, it was inevitable that Christians would see that destruction as justification for their own claims. Thus, the destruction of the Jerusalem temple enters Christian apologetic against the Jews as a sign of the way in which God has abandoned his people. This apologetic, as we shall see in our next chapter, was to have a long and interesting history.

At the same time, the symbolic meaning of the temple, namely God's presence with Israel, now finds its true realization in Jesus, the new temple, according to the developing high Christology of the Christians. In a whole range of later New Testament writings—Hebrews, Ephesians, the Fourth Gospel and the Revelation of John—this resymbolization process can be seen at work as various aspects of the Jewish cultic experience are appropriated to create a Christian symbolic world based on the Christ of faith. In Hebrews it is the rites of the Day of Atonement that find their realization in Jesus' death (Heb. 8:1–9:28); in Ephesians the exalted Christ represents the new inclusive humanity where the dividing wall that separated Jew and gentile in the temple has been broken down (Eph. 2:11–22); the Johannine Jesus, symbolically presented as the light, the bread, the lamb, the way, the source of living water, is the fulfillment not merely of the temple but of the feasts associated with it (Jn. 6, Passover; Jn. 7–8, Tabernacles; Jn. 10:22–39, Dedication); in Revelation the sufferings of the martyrs are priestly worship at the divine throne (Rev. 7), a sign of the new Jerusalem, the holy city no longer requiring a separate holy place, that would descend from on high when the final victory of the lamb is revealed (Rev. 21:1–22:4). Thus, within quite diverse social settings and in a variety of literary expressions, the temple, its cult and feasts, provided a rich field of symbolic reference for second-generation Christians, as they expressed their claims of being the true Israel, the legitimate heirs to the promise.

As well as engaging in self-definition through the appropriation and reinterpretation of Jewish symbols, the Christians had to deal with various internal problems of their own. With the violent deaths of three key figures from the earlier period—Peter, Paul and James—there was an inevitable tendency toward consolidation of the traditions stemming from them and carrying their insights further. The earliest account of the Jesus story, that of Mark, is deliberately, it would seem, open-ended in its understanding of the community and its boundaries. Gentiles, women, scribes, social outcasts—all have a place within the Christian fellowship, and the original followers, including Peter, are open to serious criticism because of their desire to set limits on who could and could not share in the community's life. But the subsequent retellings by Matthew, Luke and John are particularly conscious of the correct boundaries that need to be drawn if order is to be maintained. In the cases of Matthew and John in particular, this order is forced upon their churches precisely because of their encounters with Jewish belief that rejected the claims about Jesus.[22]

In Matthew the Christian missionaries' experience of being persecuted by Jewish synagogues is still very much alive (10:16–23), and the Old Testament memories of persecuted prophets and God's chastisement of his people are drawn on, in compensation for such treatment (23:29–36). The present hostilities toward the Matthean community are interpreted as part of a recurring cycle. In such an apologetic reading of the past the destruction of Jerusalem was inevitable (22:7; 23:39–40). Not only that, but the scribes and Pharisees, whose version of Judaism is in the process of asserting itself as authoritative for all Jews, are seriously challenged. Their inability to understand God's will emerges from their lack of knowledge of the Scriptures, giving rise to the charge of hypocrisy (ch. 23). By contrast, Jesus, the messianic teacher, knows the intimate things of God since these have been revealed to him, and he in turn has shared them with the little ones, who are at the heart of the Matthean community (11:25–27; cf. 12:6, 42). Here, vilification of the other is the key toward defining the self, and that self-definition means laying sole and privileged claim to the territory that the scribes and Pharisees also laid claim to, namely, the definitive interpretation of the divine will for Israel.

By contrast, the Johannine community's experience of Judaism was one of ongoing social contact, it would seem. Expulsion from the synagogue and a concomitant fear of the Jews seem to define the relationship. Yet the Johannine Christians refuse to become directly embroiled with synagogal Judaism (7:13; 9:22; 12:42; 16:2). The use of irony is part of a literary strategy to discredit fastidious lawabiders, as the Johannine Jesus lays claim to a higher wisdom that has echoes of Hellenistic mysticism and Philonic Judaism, although it remains rooted in the Jewish Wisdom tradition. Here the negative encounter with Judaism has built very high walls indeed around a community that has turned in on itself, not just to the exclusion of the Jews but to the rejection of the world as well. To underpin this social separatism, not to say élitism, the Johannine Christians developed the highest and most exclusive Christology of all, one that centered all revelation on Jesus, the word incarnate, to the point of reducing such important figures of Israel's history as Abraham, Moses, and Isaiah to the role of mere witnesses to Christ (4:46; 8:56; 12:41). For some Johannine Christians, this rejection of the world and devaluing of the Hebrew Scriptures was to open wide the door to Gnosticism, the most un-Jewish of all religious options, with its negative philosophy of the created order. For the same reason it was also the most un-Christian of options, as this was to emerge by the choices that were made in the second century.

Conclusion

It is time to make some concluding observations based on our historical account of Christian origins within the perspective of first-century Jewish life. In my opening remarks I discussed the need to revise some of the stereotypes that Jews and Christians have held of each other, based on misunderstandings of their own and each other's origins. It seems appropriate to address that suggestion more specifically now.

First, although the Jewish origins of early Christianity have often been acknowledged in recent discussions, there has been little exploration of the significance of such a recognition in terms of what Jews and Christians can *together* say to the modern world. Because the impasse about the messianic claims for Jesus tended to dominate Jewish-Christian dialogue, we have ignored the fact that Jews and Christians have a broader shared world-view that includes our understanding of creation, social ethics, and eschatology. In the second century both mainline Judaism and Christianity adopted a common stance against gnosticism, affirming the goodness of this world order and our responsibility for it. For other reasons, that common stance did not bring the two developing traditions any closer together then. Perhaps the current ecological crisis and nuclear threat are of such proportions to challenge us to rise above the disputes of those centuries and the mistrust based on them. Today there is an urgent need to retrieve the Hebraic understanding that human life is intimately connected with the whole of nature. This perception enjoins respect and care for the physical universe, if humans are not to destroy the world of which they are privileged to be co-creators. Secular humanist culture might be much more impressed by our religious claims if it could see signs of such concerns arising in a common witness rather than the scandal of past acrimonies being continued.

Second, my proposal does not suggest that differences did not and do not exist. Christian ecumenism has been searching, unsuccessfully, it must be said, for some model that can contain diversity in unity. One suspects, at least in the current climate of opinion, that Roman Catholicism has little tolerance for diversity and that Protestantism in general is more concerned with autonomy and difference. Yet a reading of Christian origins makes it clear that diversity in early Christian self-expression was the inevitable consequence of its rootedness within a Jewish world that tolerated diversity of religious expression within a shared understanding of being Jewish. This is a story that needs to be retold and re-examined both by Christians and Jews. The loss of the prophetic, eschatological thrust in Rabbinic Judaism coincided with its rejection of the early Christian experience based on Jesus as well as other forms of its own diverse tradition. Paradoxically, emerging Catholicism (in the sense of a universal Christian church), was also gradually to stifle the prophetic thrust that had been its own originating center, by a system of laws not unlike the Talmudic one, wedding a Jewish legalistic concern with the Stoic natural law tradition. Thus, in both traditions, the pilgrim dimension of the Israelite religion was lost in favor of a more static world-view that was intolerant of change or movement. Roman Catholics are today experiencing the life and death struggle of these two strands—the prophetic and the priestly, we may call them—within its own structures. A recognition by both Jews and Christians that to be really faithful to the past there is need to hold both strands together in a creative tension. This would provide a better framework for genuine ecumenical discussion in the context of an on-going concern for the modern world and its global problems. Such discussion would include, as of right, not just separated Christians, but Jews also who are open to learning from the diversity of their own past, part of which was expressed in the prophetic movement of Jesus the Galilean, and that still awaits its eschatological completion.

Finally, both Judaism and Christianity today need to learn that the mutual vilification we have inherited from the first common century should be understood in the context of a life-and-death debate about the proper understanding of what constituted Israel. The claim to be the sole and privileged interpreter of that center inevitably meant that walls were built on both sides and boundaries established in a sectarian manner. These were to have a distorting effect not merely on the understanding of Israel but on the understanding of the God of Israel, who has been in grave danger of becoming an idol of sectarian mentalities who claim to worship the true God. In attempting to understand the mutual vilifications of the past, we need to be aware that the rhetoric is a rhetoric of fear, based on deep-seated anxieties that cannot tolerate diversity, especially when the other that is different is very close to us. In such a climate our most strident claims to truth will inevitably victimize not liberate.

As a therapy for such attempts to destroy the other—Jew or Christian—I can think of no better prayer for Jewish-Christian dialogue today than that of Job who had also wrestled within himself with a sectarian view of God that he could no longer tolerate. When debates and the complaints are ended, Job eventually comes to rest with a new and all-encompassing vision that could serve all of us well as the proper starting point for our common search.

> I know that you can do all things
>   and that no purpose of yours can be hindered.
> I have dealt with great things that I do
>   not understand:
>   things wonderful for me that I cannot know.
> I had heard of you by word of mouth
>   but now my eye has seen you.
> Therefore I disown what I have said
>   and repent in dust and ashes (Job 42:2–6).

NOTES

1. I have found that the work of Professor Neusner provides new possibilities for Jewish-Christian dialogue, since he is prepared to examine his own tradition, using categories adopted from the Comparative Study of Religion and the History of Religions. This does not mean that his work is not subject to on-going critical evaluation, as most recently by E. P. Sanders, *Jewish Law from Jesus to the Mishnah* (Philadelphia: Trinity Press, 1990), esp. 309–33.

2. The work of David Tracy has been a considerable influence on my own

thinking in this regard, in particular his *Plurality and Ambiguity: Hermeneutics Religion and Hope* (New York: Crossroad, 1987) and more recently his *Dialogue with the Other: The Inter-Religious Dialogue,* Louvain Theological and Pastoral Monographs 1 (Louvain: Peeters Press, 1990).

3. See *The Synagogue in Late Antiquity,* ed. L. Levine (Philadelphia: ASOR/ Jewish Theological Seminary of American Publications, 1987), esp. pp. 7–32.

4. See the classic study of Martin Hengel, *Judaism and Hellenism,* 2 vols. (Philadelphia: Fortress Press, 1974), vol. 1 passim.

5. John Collins, *Between Athens and Jerusalem: Jewish Identity in the Hellenistic Diaspora* (New York: Crossroad, 1983); H. Chadwick, *Early Christian Thought and the Classical Tradition* (Oxford: Clarendon, 1987).

6. On the Essenes see Jerome Murphy O'Connor, "The Essernes and Their History," *RB* 81 (1974) 215–44, and more recently, "The Damascus Document Revisited," *RB* 92 (1984) 223–46.

7. M. Hengel, *Rabbinische Legende und Frühpharisaische Geschichte* (Heidelburg: Universitätsverlag, 1984).

8. R. Horsley and J. Hanson, *Bandits, Prophets, Messiahs: Popular Movements at the Time of Jesus* (Minneapolis: Winston Press 1985).

9. J. Neusner, *Formative Judaism: Religious and Literary Studies, Third Series. Torah, Pharisees and the Rabbis,* B.J.S. 46 (Chico, CA: Scholars Press, 1983); A. Saldarini, *Pharisees, Scribes and Sadducees in Palestinian Society* (Wilmington, DE: Glazier 1988).

10. The standard history for the period is now E. Schürer, *The History of Jewish People in the Age of Jesus Christ,* 4 vols. A New English edition revised and edited by G. Vermes, F. Millar, and M. Goodman (Edinburgh: T. & T. Clark, 1973–85). See also my *Galilee From Alexander the Great to Hadrian: A Study of Second Temple Judaism* (Wilmington, DE: Glazier/Notre Dame, 1980) and *The World of the New Testament* (Wilmington, DE: Glazier, 1981).

11. Compare, e.g., G. Vermes, *Jesus and the World of Judaism* (London: Collins, 1983), and J. Jeremias, *The Parables of Jesus* (London: S.C.M., 1972). The collection of essays by various authors, Jewish and Christian, in J. H. Charlesworth, ed., *Jesus' Jewishness: Exploring the Place of Jesus in Early Judaism* (New York: Crossroad, 1991), deals with the issues involved under a variety of aspects.

12. My *Galilee, Jesus and the Gospels: Literary Approaches and Historical Investigations* (Minneapolis: Augusburg/Fortress, 1988) attempts to develop in detail such a profile.

13. See the studies of M. Hengel, *Acts and the History of Earliest Christianity* and *Between Jesus and Paul* (Philadelphia: Fortress Press, 1979 and 1983); also B. F. Meyer, *The Early Christians: Their World Mission and Self-Discovery* (Wilmington, DE: Glazier, 1986), deals with the issues of continuity and change in a highly suggestive manner.

14. See, e.g., E. P. Sanders, *Paul and Palestinian Judaism* and *Paul, The Law, and the Jewish People* (Philadelphia: Fortress Press, 1977 and 1983); J. C. Beker, *Paul the Apostle: The Triumph of God in Life and Thought* (Philadelphia: Fortress Press, 1980).

15. J. L. Martyn, "Paul and his Jewish Christian Interpreters," *USQR* 42 (1988) 1–15 deals with this issue in a most perceptive manner, making his commentary on Galatians in the Anchor Bible Series eagerly awaited.

16. W. A. Meeks, "Breaking Away: Three New Testament Pictures of Christian-

ity's Separation from the Jewish Community," in J. Neusner and E. Frerichs, eds., *To See Ourselves as Others See Us: Christians, Jews, "Others" in Late Antiquity* (Chico, CA: Scholars Press, 1985), 93–116, esp. 104–8.

17. Freyne, *Galilee From Alexander to Hadrian*, 348–56; R. A. Pritz, *Nazarene Jewish Christianity* (Leiden: Brill 1988). The Pella tradition has been discussed most recently by C. Koester, "The Origin and Significance of the Flight to Pella Tradition," *CBQ* 51 (1989) 90–106.

18. Y. Yadin, *The Temple Scroll* (Jerusalem: IES Publications, 1984), esp. vol. 1, pp. 210ff. on column 29.

19. See, e.g., his *Messiah in Context: Israel's History and Destiny in Formative Judaism* (Philadelphia: Fortress Press 1984), 15.

20. A. Shinan, "Sermons, Targums and the Reading from Scripture in the Ancient Synagogues," in *The Synagogue in Late Antiquity*, 97–110; Lee L. Levine, *The Rabbinic Class of Roman Palestine in Late Antiquity* (Jerusalem: Yad Izhak Ben-Zvi, 1989).

21. Freyne, *Galilee, Jesus and the Gospels*, 224–39.

22. I have discussed this aspect of both gospels in detail in an essay of which the following paragraphs are a brief statement of my proposal: "Vilifying the Other and Defining the Self: Matthew's and John's anti-Jewish Polemic in Focus," in *To See Ourselves as Others See Us*, 117–44.

Jews in a Christian World: The Fourth Century

SEÁN FREYNE

IN MY PREVIOUS ESSAY I suggested that early Christianity had emerged as a prophetic apocalyptic movement, one witness among others of the great diversity of belief and practice that characterized adherents to the Jewish faith in the first century of the common era. This diversity, we saw, was attributable to social and economic as well as religious factors that had been operative within Judaism for several centuries. These factors were the direct result of the Jewish encounter with Hellenism, viewed both as a cultural mood and an economic and a social force that had radically changed the civilization patterns of the Mediterranean world.

By the end of the first century, in the wake of the destruction of the Jerusalem temple in 70 C.E., we are faced with two emerging great traditions—the one Christian, the other Pharisaic-Rabbinic—both of which began to lay rival claims to the common inheritance, to the exclusion of all others who might consider themselves to be "the true Israel." Fringe groups in both traditions, or those such as the Jewish Christians who might have acted as a bridge between them, were absorbed or pushed to one side by the developing orthodoxies on both sides. From the Christian sources in particular, we can detect actual hostility, as older, established Jewish communities who were not attracted to the new movement or its claims, exercised their social and legal clout to suppress proselytizers or expel crypto-Christians.[1] For their part Christians responded with a rhetoric of invective, borrowed from Jewish prophetic and apocalyptic literature, but suitably honed by the techniques of Hellenistic-Roman *Vituperatio.*[2]

Jews and Christians 100–300 C.E.: Some Pressing Issues

This early Christian literature might well have suffered the fate of other first century period pieces—distant echoes of struggles long ago—were it not for the fact that the Christian movement was over a period of two hundred years (100–300 C.E.) to become so successful, despite, or perhaps because of the persecutions. So successful in fact did it become that by the early fourth century it was the most obvious and suitable symbol system that could be invoked for the task of giving the empire, east and west, a sense of unity and stability after the internal and external crises of the third century. As Peter Brown, that superb historian of late antiquity expresses it, "There was nothing inevitable about the spread of Christianity; its expansion in the third century was so impressive because it had been so totally unexpected." The great persecutions of Decius (257) and Diocletian (303) are symptomatic of the threat it posed to certain established social patterns and its appeal for the developing middle classes, who found the archaic elitism of the aristocracy both alien and meaningless. When Diocletian, the soldier-emperor freed from the campaigns against marauding barbarians on the Rhine and Danube, finally established his palace at Nicomedia in 287, he was in the words of Brown, able to look out at a basilica of the Christians on the opposite hill. The Roman Empire had survived, but in this empire Christianity had come to stay.[3]

The detailed story of the development and spread of Christianity in these centuries has been told many times. Apart from a theological reading of history that sees the development as divinely ordained, the most common explanation given for the success of the early Christian movement is the fact that it was quickly able to adapt to Hellenistic thought patterns and so convince the pagan intellectual world of its claims. In this view,

Christianity's ability to shed itself of its Jewish past, and hence its strangeness and particularism as viewed by pagan outsiders, was a master stroke. Like all such generalizations, there is, of course, an element of truth in these assertions, yet they fail to grasp the complexity of the situation, and often betray false stereotypes of Judaism, Christianity, and paganism.[4]

For one thing, the fact that a lively, if acrimonious, debate between synagogue and church continued on into the fourth century shows that "the Jewish question" was not resolved at one fell swoop when second-century Christian apologists, such as Aristeides, Quadratus, and Justin, began to address Roman imperial circles directly about the truth of Christianity. These debates between Jews and Christians are real debates, even if the line of argument often sounds somewhat stilted and formal. The list of early Christian writers who produced a treatise entitled *Adversus Judaeos* is impressive—Tertullian, Cyprian, Eusebius, Augustine—among others.[5] Besides, the early Christian instructions for new converts show awareness of the need to develop one type for those with a Jewish background and another for those from paganism. It must be remembered that Judaism and Hellenism did not represent two hermetically sealed worlds, each totally separated from the other. Jews, all Jews, had for centuries been in contact with and were influenced by the Greek *geist*, as Martin Hengel and others have shown. Even when at one level that contact might appear to have been threatening, there are plenty of indications of assimilation, even in allegedly esoteric branches of Judaism. Thus, the Rabbis, writing in a strange language from the point of view of Roman paganism and debating remote issues in a style that was totally foreign to the logic of Greco-Roman schools, on closer examination can be shown to have borrowed not merely technical terms and literary forms from the larger ethos, but even some of its intellectual concerns as well. True, the idiom is thoroughly Jewish, but the issues are commonplace for that world.[6]

For its part, Greco-Roman paganism was a variegated phenomenon, a long way removed from the rationalism of classical

Athens of the fifth century B.C.E. E.R. Dodds has spoken of a
genuine loss of intellectual nerve on the part of the Greco-
Roman society of the second century.[7] Certainly, philosophical
speculation, even of the stoic variety, displays a good deal of
eclecticism, tinged to a considerable degree with religious attitudes emanating from the mystery cults. Magic, too, was popular, even for Christians and Jews, especially in Egypt, it would
seem.[8] Furthermore, the retreat into the self that gnosticism
pandered to shows the lack of harmony that many people experienced between their social lives and their own inner feelings
and searchings. Thus, the image of a hard-nosed intellectual
rationalism, anti-religious in its thrust, is anything but typical
for the world of which we speak.

While Christianity was gradually finding its way in this pagan world, how had Judaism fared in the same period? It is at
this point that one often encounters the problem of Christian
historians, both ancient and modern, operating with a definite
bias, that is betrayed by the description until recently in vogue
namely, 'late Judaism'. Far from withering up, however, Judaism, or better, some Jews in the land of Israel, whose labours
later turned out to be significant for all who would profess that
faith, had been developing an alternative system to replace the
temple as the symbolic center of Jewish faith. As described
by Jacob Neusner, this system was utopian in its outlook, a
deliberate attempt to construct a Judaism that ignored the political and historical experience of the two wars with Rome,
thereby allowing people to live their lives in the security of
their homes and villages, within stable boundaries, "on earth
as in heaven." Although fashioned by a scribal class for house-
holders and landowners, the perspective on Israel was priestly
as formulated in the Holiness Code of *Leviticus*. The code consists of a coherent world view and comprehensive way of living.
It is a world view that speaks of transcendent things—a heightened perception of the sanctification of Israel in deed and deliberation. Sanctification means two things: first, distinguishing
Israel in all its dimensions from the world in all its ways and
second, establishing the stability, predictability, order, regular-

ity, and reliability at moments and in contexts of danger. Danger means irregularity, uncertainty, betrayal. Later we shall see how in Neusner's view this utopian understanding needed to be modified in the light of Jewish experience, particularly that of the fourth century. But by the year 200 C.E., this was the vision that Rabbi Judah, the prince, had proposed for Israel, the Mishnaic system which had been maturating in the schools of Jamnia and Usha and elsewhere in Palestine for over one hundred years, building on the Pharisaic ideals of the previous century.[9]

Archaeological and other evidence for both the Diaspora and the homeland provides a different, if not contradictory picture. This suggests that the third century C.E. was a period of development and prosperity for Jews. Although they had dared to challenge for a second time the might of Rome in the Bar Cochba War (132–135 C.E.) under Hadrian, by the century's end all the old relations of tolerance for the Jewish practices enshrined in law that dated back to Julius Caesar and beyond had been restored. Rome officially recognized the Patriarch who acted as the leader of the Jewish community in terms of its internal life and external relations, and such emperors as Septimius Severus (193–211) had encouraged full Jewish participation in the city councils of the empire. A Roman historian such as Tacitus, though well informed on Jewish practices, could still pass on the current anti-Semitic vilification of Jewish origins, but a century later, another Roman historian, Dio Cassius, is much more factual and shows no such desires, although recognizing the distinctiveness of the Jews and their rebellious nature toward Rome.[10] In assessing the Jewish impact on Roman society, we must therefore avoid retrojecting the later image of the Jews living in isolated ghettoes within European cities. Jews had for a long time been learning to come to terms with paganism and had developed their own mechanisms for dealing with it, both negatively and positively. For its part, Roman paganism felt much more comfortable with Judaism than with the emerging Christian movement. As the pagan writer Celsus, writing c. 170 C.E., remarks, "at least the

Jewish worship, though peculiar, is traditional" (*Contra Celsum* 5:25).

Before we turn to the fourth century as the focus of our special attention for Jewish-Christian relations, it is important to look, however briefly, at the ways in which the sibling faith had interacted with its elder in the second and third centuries. Of course circumstances varied considerably from place to place. In Palestine and Syria the Christian community that had grown up in or close to a dominant Judaism does not appear to have fared well. Their non-participation in the Bar Cochba War undoubtedly exacerbated the situation and left Christians open to the charge of being Roman sympathizers. Justin Martyr, a Gentile born in Samaria, writing about the year 150 C.E. tells explicitly of Bar Cochba's orders to have Christians cruelly punished unless they denied Jesus as the Christ and uttered blasphemy (*1 Apology* 31). Since we know from the rabbinic writings that Bar Cochba had been acknowledged as a messianic figure by no less a person than Rabbi Aqiba, we can clearly see the religious as well as the political reasons for such persecution. Messianic claims were important on both sides, and later we shall return to that issue in more detail.

Messianism was not the only theological issue in dispute between Jews and Christians in the second century. Another very significant one was the question of the status and interpretation of the Hebrew Scriptures (the Old Testament). Although the exact limits of the canon or official list of authoritative writings may have been disputed among Jews, the principle of the authority of the sacred writings was accepted by both Jews and Christians in the first century already, even when the underlying theological reasons were quite different. By the second century, however, we can see a definite shift in the way in which those Scriptures were appealed to by Christians. To some extent the change had been forced on the Christians by such people as Marcion, a Gnostic Christian who sought to carry the Christian critique of the law, going back to Paul, to its logical conclusion by rejecting the Old Testament in its entirety as the work of the evil demiurge. Marcion had put his finger on a crucial issue that was not lost on pagan observers such as Celsus. If on the basis of the ancient Scriptures, Christians claimed to be the true heirs to Abraham's promise, thereby pointing to the antiquity of their origins, why did they not observe the laws that were written down in those Scriptures? There was no ready answer to the problem. In the first century Paul, arguing from those Scriptures, had already won for Gentile converts their freedom to live as non-Jews and yet participate fully in the life of the new movement. By the mid-second century, it had become largely a Gentile movement, and there was no reversing the trend, even if, as we shall see, the inclination to Judaize (i.e., observe Jewish customs, prayer patterns, etc.) was to continue as a live option for many Gentile converts for centuries. One answer was that the Scriptures had multiple levels of authorship, and those parts that the Christians rejected in practice could be attributed to human agency and hence jettisoned. But that would be to concede too much already to Marcion and his theory of total rejection. Use of the Scriptures as prophetic pointers to Christ, had been an essential part of early Christian apologetics in regard to Jesus; they were still crucial for the tasks of Christian catechesis in the second century. From the very beginning nothing could be conceded that would undermine the authority of those Scriptures. It was Justin Martyr, a philosopher turned Christian, who formulated the orthodox answer, based on the stoic doctrine of the *logos*, or divine reason, innate in all things. This *logos* had reached its fullest expression in Jesus, but it had equally manifested itself in the Hebrew Scriptures in all parts—ceremonial law, prophets and writings.[11]

If Christians had, in Justin's answer, the key to appropriating the whole of Scripture, the question of the irrelevance of the ceremonial and dietary laws in Christian eyes had now to be dealt with. Justin's answers are clear, if highly unflattering to the Jews. Each aspect of Jewish law—circumcision, food laws, sacrificial system, Sabbath—is shown to have been given in order to save the Jews from becoming even more perverse. These aspects of Jewish law had no intrinsic worth, but because of Jewish stubbornness and blindness, they had been imposed so that God's plan might not be totally subverted. With this kind of discussion, the argument has come a long way from Paul's view that the law is good and just and holy (Rm. 7:12) or intended as pedagogue until the fullness of time (Gal. 3:24).

While Justin writes this kind of anti-Jewish polemic in what appears to be a stylized debate with a Jew, Trypho, which could be dismissed as mere rhetoric of the schools, the reality was that Jews and Christians did meet and did debate in the real world. Origen, in accusing Celsus of introducing a fictitious Jew to discredit Christians, says that he had met and discussed issues with real Jews, who certainly did not hold the same opinions about Christians as Celsus' Jew did (*Contra Celsum* 1:41–48). There were then some possibilities for rational discussion rather than verbal abuse.[12] However, the version of Jesus' origins that circulated in Jewish circles—the son of a prostitute, who had learned magic in Egypt, etc. makes it clear that the rivalry was both real and intense.[13] A first century B.C.E. stoic philosopher, Epictetus, could list Jews among the viable religious options of the Roman world together with Egyptians and Syrians, suggesting that Judaism was viewed by some enlightened pagans in a similar light to the Isis and Cybele cults that had come to Rome from the East. Later pagan philosophers such as Galen and Porphyry saw real philosophical worth in the writings of Moses ("What else is Plato except Moses speaking Attic?" as Numenius of Apamea phrases it). Within the neo-Platonic Pantheon, the Jewish God had an important if not absolute position as ruler of the created universe. This is the foreground against which we are to understand the rival claims of proselytizing Jews and Christians. It was in the interests of both sides that the God of the Hebrew Scriptures be recognized as both powerful and philosophically respectable. At the same time, neither side was prepared to concede legitimacy to the other as interpreter of that God for others who might be interested in professing him. One such pagan was

Constantine, the heir apparent to control of the West, as he prepared for a confrontation with Maxentius in 311 C.E.

A Changing World: Constantine, Jews and Christians

The view of Constantine that has prevailed is that of the saintly figure, the first Christian Emperor. His "conversion," prior to the victory at the Milvian Bridge that made him undisputed master of the Western empire, has been hailed as an event more momentous for the future of Christianity than even Paul's experience on the road to Damascus. Yet, not even Eusebius, Constantine's earliest biographer, who initiated the legendary picture could disguise the fact that the decision to opt for the Christian God as the Supreme God—after consideration of the fate of his various predecessors and the gods they had invoked as their patrons—had considerable political implications. The fact that Constantine continued to have the image of the solar god on his coins even after 324, as well as the terms of the edict of Milan, which gave toleration to other religious groups in the empire as well as to Christianity, shows that he was keeping his options open, both religiously and politically.[14] Even the emperor's direct intervention in the Council of Nicea must be seen against the background of his desire to maintain political and economic stability in the East, now that he had achieved the status of the sole emperor of the Roman world after the removal of Licinius, the viceroy in the East, in 323. Christians by their sheer numbers had attained such a level of social and political importance that their internal disputes could be disruptive of the whole social order.

In contrast to this understanding of Constantine by later Christian hagiographers and historians alike, the prevailing Jewish view has been that with the advent of the Christian empire, Jews were inevitably committed to being exiles even in their own land—the so-called "lachrymose view" of Jewish history. However, a careful review of the legal status of Jews as revealed in the Theodotian Code (a collection of various imperial decrees and letters from Constantine to Theodotius II) does not substantiate this view. There is no serious evidence of a gradual deterioration of the Jewish position in the various enactments, either those by Constantine or by other Christian emperors after his death, until well into the fifth century.[15] On some issues, such as the prohibition on visiting Jerusalem on the ninth of Ab to mourn its destruction, dating from the Bar Cochba revolt, there seems to have been a relaxation. Privileges of the Jewish patriarchs and elders were retained, even though these were extended to Christian clergy also. As late as 393 C.E. Theodotius I had issued a rescript to the East declaring that "the sect of the Jews is forbidden by no law." This is highly significant in view of the fact that in 388 Christian monks at Callinicum on the Euphrates had instigated the burning of a synagogue. Although Theodotius had originally ordered the rebuilding of the synagogue and the punishment of the monks he had relented under pressure from the powerful bishop of Milan, Ambrose.[16]

Several different explanations have been given for this situation. Some have seen the tolerance of, if not leniency towards the Jews, as influenced by the needs of Christian apologetics. Unlike other rival, pagan groups, Christians needed the continued survival of Judaism, but in a subservient position, as part of their own claims to be an ancient and true religion. Others explain imperial policy as part of a general Roman respect for ancient laws and customs, coupled with a philosophical tolerance of diverse religious traditions that saw the many different forms of religious practice as local expressions of worship of the Supreme God, who was ultimately unknowable. More recently, the case has been well argued for the continued influence of the Jews within the Roman Empire as a social and political force.[17] A number of converging lines of evidence shows how real this factor was in the latter half of the fourth century. Already in 351, there had been a revolt in Palestine, lead by one Patricius, probably based on messianic hopes, and this had taken some time and energy, as well as manpower that could have been deployed elsewhere, to quell. Memories of the wars of 66–70 and 132–135 C.E. must have been revived for the Romans. Despite this disturbance, the archaeological evidence from Galilee in particular shows considerable prosperity on the part of Jewish communities there, undisturbed throughout the fourth century.[18] In addition, the evidence from a fourth century pagan writer, Libanius of Antioch, as well as from the Theodotian Code shows that the Patriarch of the Jews in Palestine was recognized as a powerful and influential character, well versed in the ways of the Roman world of the time and as somebody who had to be respected, even by the emperor, despite his having violated imperial edicts. The fact that the Patriarch presided over a Jewish population, a large portion of which lived outside the confines of the empire in Persia, made his position all the more sensitive in imperial eyes.

Whatever the reasons may have been, it seems fair to suggest that the first Christian century was not an unmitigated disaster for Jews in the Roman Empire. Presently, we shall discuss the Julian affair and its importance for Christian attitudes toward Judaism. Yet, for all the external signs that nothing had changed for Jews, Jacob Neusner's recent studies suggest that profound changes were taking place within Judaism. Neusner bases this view on analysis of the Jewish sources from the fourth century. The authors of Rabbinic commentaries on the books of Genesis and Leviticus entitled *Genesis Rabbah* and *Leviticus Rabbah* see in the Jacob-Esau story a type of the Jew-Roman relationship, since at that time Rome itself in Jewish eyes was both a religious (i.e., Christian) as well as a political reality. Rome was no longer just another hostile pagan force, as in earlier Jewish writings, but a brother whose deceptive nature was all the more insidious.[19] Corresponding to this awareness of the religious dimensions of the political change, Neusner finds that the Rabbinic literature emanating from fourth century Palestine, the *Yerushalmi*, or Palestinian Talmud, as well as the Biblical commentaries just mentioned, show a very definite theological development from earlier documents.[20] Two areas in particular stand out—eschatology, with special emphasis on the Messiah, and the role of the Scriptures in defining the symbol of the

Torah. Both had already surfaced in Jewish-Christian debates in previous centuries, as we have seen, but now they have a great actuality on the Jewish side.

After the failure of the Bar Cochba revolt with its messianic orientation, the developing tradition of the Mishnah seems to have deliberately ignored the messianic hopes for an ultimate national salvation. Sanctification, in the sense of a personal striving to live out the rabbinic ideal of piety through deeds of loving kindness, rather than awaiting the coming of the Messiah as a savior figure was the goal, according to Mishnah *Sotah* 9:9–15. The gnostic systems of the second century could have their various redeemer myths, and the Christians could continue to develop a high Christology with the aid of Greek philosophy, but the Mishnaic system was to leave the messianic idea systemically inert, as it formulated another way of holiness. By the fourth century, however, the Messiah figure returns in various guises in *Yerushalmi*, itself a commentary on the Mishnah. The framers of the Talmud hoped for the coming of the Messiah in their own day, and his coming would mean salvation in terms of resurrection to the new age for those who had been faithful to the Mishnaic ideal.[21] In particular, the search for suitable criteria for the Messiah's identification suggests some pressing concerns of the day, a glimpse of which may be captured in the revolt of Patricius under Gallus. Christian messianism was also finding a new expression in the description of Constantine and his achievements by Eusebius. In the *Historia Ecclesiastica* (9:9–7) the battle of the Milvian Bridge is depicted in terms reminisent of the exodus, but in the *Triennial Oration* to celebrate the thirtieth anniversary of the event, the apotheosis of Constantine is virtually complete—an embodiment of the eternal logos, destined to complete his reign on earth.[22] The Christ-victim becomes the Christ-victor in the career of Constantine.

The authority and meaning of the Hebrew Scriptures had now become a central question on the Jewish side also. The Mishnah had built its program on the foundation of the Biblical or, more precisely, the priestly view of Israel, but it had done so without explicit reference to those Scriptures. The first apologists for the Mishnah in tractate *Aboth* (circa 250 C.E.) had developed the idea of the oral Torah coming from Moses to the rabbis of the present generation via the men of the great synagogue. Their words then have equal authority with the written Scriptures, which meanwhile the Christians were claiming to interpret correctly through their Christological and typological hermeneutics. By the fourth century, however, something more was at stake in regard to those Scriptures. If the Jewish sages of the second and third centuries chose to ignore Christian claims that they did not understand their own Scriptures, now in the fourth, their successors, the Palestinian sages, offered the definitive interpretation of those texts in line with the Mishnaic point of view, through a deliberate point by point reference to the Scriptures, something the framers of Mishnah had themselves ignored.[23] Once again, it is possible to suggest as one reason for this aggressive reappropriation of the Scriptures the fact that Christians applied them to the immediate post-Constantinian situation. Those Scriptures were being used now to validate and interpret Constantine's victories. It is the warriors David and Moses who are embodied in the portrayal, in contrast to Rabbi David and Rabbi Moses of the *Yerushalmi* portrayal. Indeed, this deliberate casting of Constantine in the role of the Old Testament conquering figures was soon to be given conscious expression in the land of Israel itself. Mamre, the site hallowed by the Patriarch Abraham, was developed as a Christian shrine, thus supporting the view Eusebius provides elsewhere that Constantine's rule revived the universal age of the Patriarchs, whom he portrays as Christians before Christ. It is in the changing sacral landscape itself, rather than in the alleged anti-Judaic legislation of Constantine and his successors that we can best capture what is really at issue between Jews and Christians in the fourth century.

Both the temple and the land, as its extension, had been central symbols of Jewish election since Israelite days. In our previous essay we saw that the critique of the Jesus movement was directed against the absolutizing of these symbols in Second

Temple Judaism, and that critique had been developed theologically within early Christianity, as various aspects of the temple and its cult provided a suitable field of symbolic reference for interpreting Jesus. The destruction of the Jerusalem temple had further aided the Christian apologetic task, as detailed descriptions of the event, cast in the form of prophecy, are put on the lips of Jesus by later evangelists, such as Luke and Matthew. By the fourth century, the continued exclusion of the Jews from Jerusalem and the fact that the temple had not been rebuilt were central pillars of the Christian claim that, with the rejection of Jesus, the Jews had lost their privileged position in God's plan for Israel. In the intervening centuries, however, Christians were in no position to lay counter claims to temple or land, nor did their apologetic needs demand such. With Constantine's victory this situation was to change.

We are dependent on Eusebius for the interpretation that Christians were likely to put on the building of the Church of the Holy Sepulchre at Jerusalem and other Christian churches throughout the Holy Land, especially in Jerusalem itself. There is some evidence from earlier centuries to suggest that Christians inspired by the image of the new Jerusalem of the Book of Revelation had hoped that the Second Coming would take place in Jerusalem. Thus, despite Hadrian's aggressive paganization, a Christian community with its own church had continued there. Now, however, it was possible to "discover" the tomb of the Savior right in the center of Hadrian's forum underneath a shrine of Venus (Eusebius) or Jupiter (Jerome). Constantine had the whole area excavated, thus removing the pagan symbols, and he erected a basilica, since the discovery of the exact site "surpassed all astonishment" for the emperor (*Vita Constantini* iii 28, 301). For him the discovery was another sign of the divine favor with which his reign was blessed.

For Jews who went up to mourn the loss of the temple on the 9th of Ab, however, it must have been a rather depressing experience to realize that the hated symbols of paganism on Aelia Capitolina, which had given rise to the Bar Cochba War two centuries earlier, only now had to give way to a Christian basilica that celebrated the victory of Christianity and their own relegation in the divine plan. The dedication ceremony was a lavish occasion, attended by bishops from all over the East, brought there at state expense. The event coincided with the thirtieth year of Constantine's reign 335 and was intended to be a fitting triumphal celebration with largesse freely distributed to the poor. From the account of the dedicatory speech that Eusebius delivered at a similar function at Tyre, we can capture something of the thinking that lay behind the architecture of these edifices. They were essentially pilgrim churches, where the physical layout recalled the gradual progress of the faithful from ignorance through purification and instruction, until finally arriving at the Holy of Holies. The spiritual temple that Christians had used as a symbol of their personal and communal life of faith (1 Cor. 3:10ff; Eph. 2:20–22), now took on concrete expression (if you will pardon the pun!) in these impressive buildings. The symbol of the new Jerusalem was now an actuality for Christians, who quickly began to flock to Palestine on pilgrimage, to visit the sites hallowed by the events of the Savior's life. Spiritual symbolism and religious geography have come together to exclude the Jews from their own sacred sites, especially the temple mount of Jerusalem.[24]

In view of this rapid Christianization of the Holy Land, we can sense something of the shock to the Christian self-confidence that was caused by the emperor Julian's attempt to reverse the whole Constantinian achievement only thirty years later. Julian is one of the truly fascinating figures of antiquity, the last of the Helenes. His program of restoring pagan religion—with special emphasis on Helios, the Sun God, to its rightful place as the religion of the empire—was, to say the least, ambitious. Yet this very program held out a ray of hope for Jews, it would seem, even though there is no direct trace of this in the Jewish writings of the period. As an apostate Christian, Julian knew the Christian argument from the inside, and how it had been constructed on the edifice of the shattered ruins of Jerusalem. His decision to have the temple at Jerusalem rebuilt must surely be seen against this background.[25] Julian excluded the Christians from teaching in the pagan schools, but he did not dare destroy the buildings of Constantine. For his purposes, however, nothing could better symbolize the challenge to Christian claims than to have the Jerusalem temple rebuilt, alongside the Constantinian symbol of Christ's victory, especially the Church of the Holy Sepulchre, in view of Christian reliance on the gospel prophecies about the temple's destruction. In his *Contra Galilaeos* Julian makes it quite clear that despite his espousal of the Jewish God, he was not becoming a Jew. His god was the Supreme God, Helios, of which the Hebrew Scriptures spoke, but whom the Jews did not recognize or know. His espousal of the Jewish God to the discredit of the Christian claims may well have been recognized for what it was by the sages, yet the actual beginning of work on the Temple Mount can scarcely have gone unnoticed by the Jewish population, for whom the site was still a sacred place.[26]

In one sense Julian's attack on the Christian position was flattering, though it certainly was not seen in that light by his Christian contemporaries. Apparently the work was impeded by an earthquake and finally terminated when Julian perished in his war against the Persians on the eastern frontier. It takes little imagination to perceive the way in which Christians were likely to interpret such events. The hand of God was clearly at work in preventing this outrageous insult to his plan from taking place. Jerome, Rufinus, Ephrem, but especially John Chrysostom, are Christian writers who reacted with horror, shock, and relief at the project and its failure. Robert Wilken's recent impressive study of John Chrysostom whose homilies against the Jews are the high point of early Christian, anti-Jewish invective,[27] has shown how deep an impact the Julian affair had left on Christian consciousness of the following century. Five times he returns to the theme, only to insist that the failure of the enterprise shows clearly that the Christian apologetic was true and that Christ's divinity was intact, based on his predictions about Jerusalem and its temple.[28] What is highly significant about Wilken's analysis is that as late as the early part of the fifth century there were Judaizing Christians at Antioch who frequented the synagogue and who dearly hoped for such a restoration of Judaism. John's homilies are directed to these rather than to the Jews as such. Clearly, some Christians still found the ambiance of the synagogue a proper nurturing place for their faith, but for John such a compromise would invalidate Christian claims about Christ. Christology, even at Antioch, could not get away from the Jewish question.

The temple was the focal point of the land according to the Pentateuchal view, and so in the fourth century it is not surprising to find the beginnings of the idea of a Christian Holy Land corresponding to the Christian temple. Christian monks flocked to Palestine to people the deserts that had been made holy by Elijah, John, and Jesus. Christian churches dotted the landscape, and Christian pilgrims came from all over the Empire to visit the holy places of their faith.[29] Christian writers and commentators on the Biblical prophecies of restoration (e.g., Isaiah, Ezekiel, and Zechariah) from previous centuries had shown no interest in the application of these texts to the earthly Jerusalem and its land. Now, however, the attitudes have decidedly changed. Palestine and Jerusalem were important to Christians and such biblical commentators as Jerome, Theodoret of Cyr, and others were at pains to combat current Jewish views on these issues.[30] It is their holy land, and any resurgence of Jewish messianism that would envisage a historical restoration of Jews would be threatening in the extreme. Not only did the ruined temple confirm Christian claims but also a Christian holy land was the sign of God's triumph in Christ. That Jewish hopes in the coming of the Messiah showed a definite upturn in this century is hardly surprising since the belief was that the restoration of Israel could only take place when the Messiah would come. The revolt of Patricius under Gallus may well have had its base in such an upsurge of expectation and speculation. Certainly, the need for restoration was now more acute than ever before as Christians laid open and obvious claims to the very land of Israel, backed by the might of Rome.

In addition to the Messiah and the Scriptures, there is now

a third symbol in dispute between Jews and Christians, namely the land itself as the visible and tangible signs of the promises. By laying claim to the land, Christians profoundly changed the way in which they perceived themselves, and not in the most decidedly Christian of ways when viewed by the standards of the first century.[31] The emphasis was on the historical realization of the symbols—temple, Torah, and land, and hence the loss of their symbolic power to evoke wider horizons, and deeper feelings than those that control of and patronage by the Roman Empire could offer. Somewhat uneasily at first, but later with a confident enthusiasm in God's plans for history, Christianity was about to settle down with the power of Rome. The symbiosis of the lamb and the lion had occurred in a way that Isaiah would not necessarily have approved.

Conclusion

The issues of Messiah, Temple and Land, and Torah are still with us in terms of Jewish and Christian dialogue today. The lines that were taking shape in the fourth century are still the demarcating lines of these two world religions in a way that first century issues are not. Does our account of the way these issues came to the fore offer any possibility that it might have been otherwise? What lessons can we learn, and how can we improve relationships on both sides in the light of our account?

Rosemary Reuther in her book *Faith and Fratricide* has argued that based on its messianic doctrine, Christianity is inherently anti-Jewish. True, the messianic issue was of vital importance to all Christian believers from the start, but it did not mean that they all thereby abandoned their Judaism. What happened to the messianic idea among Christians in the fourth century did certainly mean that the Messiah myth became so rooted in a position of Christian dominance, at the expense of the Jews, that no mutual grounds for understanding might appear to exist subsequently. It is for Christians to evaluate how far the development of the messianic doctrine in terms of the Trinitarian and Christological debates at Nicea, Constantinople, and Chalcedon are the inherent development of their own earlier beliefs in Jesus going back to the New Testament, or are, in part at least, ideologically motivated in line with the needs of a triumphant Christianity of the fourth century. In the light of the above discussion, it would seem appropriate to suggest that some revision of this picture is possible. Certainly, many contemporary Christologians are less than happy with those later formulations, and there is a growing awareness of the need to retrieve for Christology some of the relational and eschatological images of the New Testament language as a counterbalance to the static, philosophical categories of the later debates and conciliar statements. Jews can help us to understand what the Messiah myth stood for within Judaism, recognizing for their part that the political overtones of this belief need not, and in fact were not, always essential to it. If the eschatological nature of the Messiah myth were to become central to contemporary discussions, it would not thereby eliminate all differences between the two religions, but it would help us both to be aware of what the myth originally claimed, namely God's ultimate and final act of redemption for the human family, which, despite our various claims, is still the hope of both religious traditions at their best. Liberation theology today is finding in the crucified-Messiah story of the Christians not the symbol of dominance and oppression that it became with the Constantinian triumph but rather the symbol of God's solidarity with the poor and oppressed. Perhaps it is not too much to hope that this discovery of the basic meaning of the symbol as professed by first-century Christians, might also function to free us from our ideologies of dominance and control, thereby discovering a new sense of solidarity in a common hope with our Jewish brothers and sisters.

Were we to have such a vision as our starting point, the meaning of the other symbols for both traditions could be suitably revised. Both Jews and Christians have used the Hebrew Scriptures for their own ends, as our perusal of fourth-century attitudes has revealed. Christians opted for a Christological reading of the prophets and suitably ignored the law, or those parts of it that they no longer wished to practice, while maintaining, contrary to Marcion, that the whole of Tanach or scriptures was equally important. Jews built their vision on the priestly ideal and were less concerned with the prophets, except insofar as they could be invoked to support their particular perspective. Written texts from the past are always read out of particular contexts, and those contexts determine what is found important and disclosive of meaning for life at any given epoch. It is this quality of being able to be disclosive of ultimate meaning in different contexts, that gives our Scriptures the character of a religious classic, as David Tracy reminds us. The fact that Jews and Christians have read their common classic differently and found different parts of it more significant will always warn us that our experiences are different and that such pluralism of readings can be enriching not divisive, provided we are willing to operate with a hermeneutic of suspicion, aware of how our apologetic needs determine our particular perspective. Yet, if we were really convinced that in the Hebrew Scriptures we did have a common text of classic proportions, we might more freely let go of our ideological impositions on that text and allow it to challenge even our most cherished claims.

For Jews one such cherished claim based on the Hebrew Scriptures is that of the land. As Robert Wilken says, in the fourth century Jews and Christians found another issue to fight about in the issue of the land. It is an issue that is tragically with us still. The very fact that the same Scriptures that are called on to support the land as a religious symbol also describe the condition of exile has given some Jews pause with regard to the modern state of Israel and the religious claims that are sometimes based on its existence. At the same time Christians must learn that the sense of dominance and triumph to which the fourth century Christianization of the Holy Land gave concrete expression, was the beginning of an ideological Christianity whose very conduct towards Jews over the centuries has, as a sign of its own bad conscience, made the modern state of Israel a political, if not a religious, necessity. Until the time of Constantine, Christians found the image of the new Jerusalem

a suitable spatial symbol to express their sense of an eschatological coming together of Jew and Gentile as one people in
God's design. That vision is also expressed in terms of the temple imagery in the epistle to the Ephesians, whose author views
the destruction of the Jerusalem temple not as a sign of condemnation for Jews but as a sign of hope that the dividing wall
of separation has now finally been broken down and that those
who were "strangers and afar" can now draw near (Eph. 2:14).
It is time for us to begin to implement that vision. We have
built too many other dividing walls in the interim.

NOTES

1. Mt. 10:16–23; 23:23–33; Jn. 9:22; 16:2; 1 Thess. 2:16–20; Rev. 2:9–10; 3:9.

2. See my article "Vilifying the Other and Defining the Self: Matthew's and
John's Anti-Jewish Polemic in Focus," in To See Ourselves as Others See Us:
Christians, Jews, "Others" in Late Antiquity, ed. J. Neusner and E. Frerichs (Chico,
CA: Scholars Press, 1985); A. Yarbro Collins, "Vilification and Self-Definition in
the Book of Revelation," in Christians Among Jews and Gentiles, ed. G. W. Nick-
elsburg and G. MacRae (Philadelphia: Fortress Press, 1980), 308–20.

3. The Making of Late Antiquity (London: Thames & Hudson, 1971), 49–68.
See also Robin Lane Fox, Pagans and Christians (Penguin Books, 1988), 285–335.

4. See R. MacMullan, Christianising the Roman Empire A.D. 100–400 (New
Haven: Yale University Press, 1984).

5. A. L. Williams, Adversus Judaeos (Cambridge: Cambridge University
Press, 1932).

6. H. Fischel, Rabbinic Literature and Greco-Roman Philosophy: A Study of
Epicurea and Rhetorica in Early Midrashic Writings (Leiden: Brill, 1973).

7. See also R. MacMullan, Paganism in the Roman Empire (New Haven and
London: Yale University Press, 1981).

8. See P. Alexander in E. Schürer, The History of the Jewish People in the Age
of Jesus Christ, 4 vols. Revised and edited G. Vermes, F. Millar, M. Black (Edinburgh,
T. & T. Clark, 1973–8), vol. 3, pp. 342–79.

9. J. Neusner, Judaism: The Evidence of the Mishnah (Chicago: Chicago University Press, 1981), esp. ch. 6. For a critique of Neusner, often sharply polemical
and with very different presuppositions, see E. P. Sanders, Jewish Law from Jesus
to the Mishnah (London: S.C.M. Press, 1990), 309–31. See also A. Paul, "La Torah
et le Canon Chrétien: Deux Suppléances d'un Manque Politique," RSR 71 (1983)
139–47.

10. John Gager, The Origins of Anti-Semitism (Oxford: Oxford University
Press, 1983).

11. H. van Compenhausen, *The Formation of the Christian Bible* (Philadelphia: Fortress Press, 1972), 62–102; H. Chadwick, "Justin Martyr's Defense of Christianity," *BJRL* 47 (1965) 275–97.

12. N. de Lange, *Origen and the Jews: Studies in Jewish Christian Relations in Third Century Palestine* (Cambridge: Cambridge University Press, 1976).

13. E. Bammel, "Christian Origins in Jewish Tradition," *NTS* 13 (1966) 317–35; W. Horbury, "The Benediction of the *Minim* and Early Jewish-Christian Controversy," *JTS* 33 (1982) 19–61.

14. See R. M. Grant, *Religion and Politics at the Council of Nicea*, Inaugural Lecture, Chicago Divinity School, 1973, and E. A. Judge, *The Conversion of Rome*, Macquarie Ancient History Association No. 1 (Macquarie University, North Ryde, Australia 1980), based on the papyrological evidence, mainly from Egypt.

15. R. Wilken, "The Jews and Christian Apologetics after Theodosius I *Cunctos Populos*," *HTR* 73 (1980) 451–71, esp. 465f.

16. See B. Bachrach, "The Jewish Community of the Later Roman Empire as seen in the *Codex Theodosianus*," in *To See Ourselves as Others See Us*, 399–421, esp. 402–8.

17. Barbara Geller Nathanson, "Jews, Christians and the Gallus Revolt in Fourth-Century Palestine," *BA* (1986) 26–36.

18. See most recently E. Meyers, "Early Judaism and Christianity in the Light of Archaeology," *BA* 51 (1988) 69–89 for a brief statement of his more scholarly publications dealing with the excavations in Upper Galilee, especially the synagogues.

19. J. Neusner, *From Sibling to Enemy* (Providence, RI: Brown University Publications, 1987).

20. See in particular his *Judaism and Christianity in the Age of Constantine* (Chicago: Chicago University Press, 1987).

21. J. Neusner, *Messiah in Context: Israel's History and Destiny in Formative Judaism* (Philadelphia: Fortress Press, 1984).

22. See A. Kee, *Constantine versus Christ* (London: S.C.M. Press 1982), 27–34; H. A. Drake, *A Historical Study and New Translation of Eusebius' Triennial Oration* (Berkley: University of California Press, 1973).

23. It is one of Jacob Neusner's major contributions to the study of Judaism in Antiquity to have suggested the apologetic and theological concerns of the various Jewish writings in terms of a developing and changing system. In addition to his works already cited, see also his *Judaism in Society: The Evidence of Yerushalmi: Towards a Natural History of Religion* (Chicago: Chicago University Press, 1983).

24. R. Wilken, "Byzantine Palestine: A Christian Holy Land," *BA* 51 (1988) 214–18 and 233–37.

25. Y. Levy, "Julian the Apostate and the Building of the Temple," in *Jerusalem Cathedra* 3, ed. L. Levine (Jerusalem: Magnes Press), 70–96.

26. R. Wilken, *The Christians as the Romans Saw Them* (New Haven: Yale University Press, 1984), 164–96.

27. W. Meeks and R. Wilken, *Jews and Christians in Antioch*, SBL Sources for Biblical Study 13 (Missoula, MT: Scholars Press, 1978), with an English translation of the homilies.

28. R. Wilken, *John Chrysostom and the Jews: Rhetoric and Reality in the Late Fourth Century* (Berkley: University of California Press, 1983).

29. For archaeological evidence of early Christian Churches in Palestine see *Bib-*

lical Archaeologist 51 (1988) number 4: M. Piccirillo, "The Mosaics at Um er-Rasas in Jordan," 208–14 and 227–31; R. Schnick, "Christian Life in Palestine during the Early Islamic Period," 218–22; B. de Vries, "Jordan's Churches in Their Urban Context in Late Antiquity," 222–26.

30. R. Wilken, "The Restoration of Israel in Biblical Prophecy: Christian and Jewish Responses in the Early Byzantine Period," in *To See Ourselves as Others See Us*, 443–71.

31. See E. Fascher, "Jerusalems Untergang in der Urchristlichen und alt-kirchlichen Uberlieferung," *Theol. Lit. Zeitung* 89 (1964) 82–98.

The Lives of the Saints
and the Pursuit of Virtue

ROBERT L. WILKEN

OF THE SEVERAL PATHS that lead to virtue, the broadest and the most obliging is the way of imitation. By observing the lives of holy men and women and imitating their deeds, we become virtuous. Before we can become doers, we first must be spectators. Origen, the fecund Christian teacher from ancient Alexandria, said, "Genuine transformation of life comes from reading the ancient Scriptures, learning who the just were and *imitating* them," to which he shrewdly appended the caveat, and "learning who were reproved and guarding against falling under the same censure."[1]

In a scene in *The Brothers Karamazov*, shortly before Father Zosima dies, the aged monk gathers his fellow monks and friends in his cell for a final conversation. As a child he had owned a book with beautiful pictures entitled *A Hundred and Four Stories from the Old and the New Testaments*. From this book he had learned to read and, as an old man, he still keeps it on his shelf. Father Zosima remembers many tales from it as well as other stories of good and holy men and women; stories of Job and Esther and Jonah, the parables of Jesus, the conversion of Saul, and lives of the saints Alexel and Mary of Egypt—stories that plant a tiny mysterious seed in the hearts of men and women. Some of these "sacred tales," like the story of Job, he cannot read "without tears." Like a bright spark amidst darkness, or a seed that never dies, these accounts lodge indelibly in his memory. In these stories of God's people, says

55

Father Zosima, one "beh[olds] God's glory." He asks, "What is Christ's word without an example?"[2]

Without examples, without imitation, there can be no human life or civilization, no art or culture, no virtue or holiness. The elementary activities of fashioning a clay pot or constructing a cabinet, learning to speak or sculpting a statue have their beginning in the imitation of what others do. This atavistic truth is as old as humankind, but in the West it was the Greeks who helped us understand its place in the moral life. And in classical antiquity it is nowhere displayed with greater art than in Plutarch's *Lives*.

"Our senses," wrote Plutarch, "apprehend the things they encounter simply because of the impact they make upon us. For this reason the senses must receive everything that presents itself whether it be useful or useless. The mind, however, has the power to turn itself away if it wishes, and readily fasten on what seems best. It is proper, then, that it pursue what is best, so that it may not only behold it but also be nourished by beholding it. . . . Our spiritual vision must be applied to such objects that by their charm invite it to attain its proper good."

Plutarch continued, "Such objects are to be found in *virtuous deeds*; for these implant in those who search them out a zeal and yearning that leads to imitation. In other cases, admiration of the deed does not at once lead to an impulse to do it. Indeed, in many cases the contrary is true. We take delight in what is produced, but have no desire to imitate the one who produced it." We may take pleasure in, for example, the product of a carpenter or factory worker without wanting to be like them. Their actions generate no "ardor in the breast to imitate" their labor, "nor any buoyancy in the soul that arouses zealous impulses to do likewise. But virtue [arete] disposes a person so that as soon as one admires the works of virtue one strives to emulate those who performed them. The good things of fortune we love to possess and enjoy, those of virtues we love to perform. . . . The good creates a stir of activity towards itself and implants at once in the spectator an impulse toward action."[3]

In writing the lives of noble Greeks and Romans, Plutarch

gave literary form to ideas and conceptions that reached back into Greek antiquity and that continued to exercise a spell over moralists in the early empire. It was a simple yet profound truth, acknowledged by all, even those who chose another vehicle for moral formation. Plutarch's contemporary Seneca, a Stoic philosopher (Plutarch was an eclectic Platonist), wrote letters and moral essays. In one of many letters to Lucilius, a youth he hoped to mold, Seneca wrote: "Plato, Aristotle, and the whole throng of sages ... derived more benefit from the *character* than from the words of Socrates. The way is long if one follows precepts, but short and accommodating if one imitates examples."[4]

Long before Plutarch and Seneca, Aristotle had shown that the pursuit of virtue is indissolubly bound to deeds, that good actions are not simply the *end* toward which one strives, but the *means* to reach the goal. It is only through the repeated performance of good deeds that a virtuous life is possible. In Aristotle's famous formulation, "We become just by doing just acts, temperate by doing temperate acts, brave by doing brave acts."[5] From this conception it was only a short step to the idea that character could be deduced from actions; hence a narrative (selective to be sure) of a person's actions (i.e., a life—*bios* in Greek) was an indulgent instrument for engendering virtue. The philosophical grounding for the writing of lives rested on this intimate bond between "deeds" *(praxeis)* and character *(ethos)*.[6] And, as Plutarch recognized, deeds need not mean great and noble displays of bravery or courage. "A slight thing, like a phrase or a jest," he wrote, is often more revealing of character than "battles where thousands fall." For character has to do with constancy and steadiness.[7]

By the time Christianity made its appearance in the Roman Empire, the practice of writing lives was well established.[8] Yet Christian hagiography, if we wish to use the later term, did not emerge until the end of the third century and did not burst into luxurious bloom until the fifth. There are, of course, "tales" of heroic men and women in the apocryphal acts of the apostles (as well as in the canonical Acts), and the early acts of the martyrs narrate the "deeds" of a martyr's final hours or days.[9] And most important of all, there is the life par excellence, the life of Jesus, displayed with subtlety of perception and refinement of feeling in the gospels, to which I will return shortly.

The initial impression one receives, however, from early Christian literature is that the vehicle of moral instruction is the *precept*.[10] In the earliest Christian writing (1 Thessalonians, for example), Paul said: "You know what *precepts* we gave you through the Lord Jesus. For this is the will of God your sanctification; that you abstain from unchastity; that each one of you know how to take a wife for himself . . . that no man transgress and wrong his brother in this matter." Sprinkled throughout the New Testament are other lists of precepts, some simple imperatives to refrain from "anger, wrath, malice, slander, foul talk," and graceful and polished aphorisms constructed on the model of the book of Proverbs or the Wisdom of Sirach ("Let every person be quick to hear, slow to speak, slow to anger") and "If anyone thinks he is religious, and does not bridle his tongue but deceives his heart, this man's religion is vain."[11]

Often the precepts stand alone, but in places they are buttressed by examples: Job as an example of "steadfastness" (James 5:11), Abraham the model of faith (Heb. 11:8), and Elijah as evidence of the power of the prayer of the righteous (James 5:17). In the gospels Jesus conscripted living persons as examples, a certain poor widow who offered a farthing, little children, Mary of Bethany, the centurion whose slave was at the point of death, and, of course, he told stories and parables, sometimes ending with the words: "Go thou and do likewise" (Luke 10:37). From the beginning the idea of imitation shaped Christian moral discourse.[12] Paul entreated the Corinthians to take him as an example: "I urge you, then, be imitators of me" (1 Cor. 4:16). Long before the advent of Christianity, the principle was endorsed by Jews, in, for example, the roll call of heroes in the section "let us now praise famous men" in the Wisdom of Sirach (44 ff.). In Christianity the book of Hebrews unfolds a roster of men and women of faith in chapter eleven—

Abel, Enoch, Noah, Abraham, Sarah, Moses, Rahab, Gideon—
and 1 Clement produces another list.[13]

Examples, however, are not lives. In the case of the biblical
heroes, holy men and women tend to function more as types,
i.e., instances of particular virtues, than as iridescent models.
In Ambrose's classical work on Christian ethics, *De Officiis*,
Abraham illustrates prudence; Susanna, modesty; David, courage; Job, patience.[14] Stripped of the grainy texture of place and
time, the saints of the distant past become pallid and lackluster,
mobilized too often for too many different purposes. As graphic
as the saints' deeds may once have been, repeated appeal to the
same figures divests them of the very features that once made
them noteworthy, severing the emotional bond between doer
and spectator.

Why, then, no lives? The most obvious reason was that the
gospels stood in the way. The supreme model for Christian life
was Jesus: "I have given you an example that you also should
do as I have done" (John 13:15). Even those whose exploits
would have been fit subjects for a life—most notably Peter and
Paul (an idea the author of Acts no doubt contemplated, and in
part executed)—looked to Jesus. "Be imitators of me," wrote
Paul, "as I am of Christ" (1 Cor. 11:1). Others followed in this
wake. Ignatius of Antioch exhorted the Philadelpians "to imitate Jesus Christ as he imitated the Father." Jesus' call to disci-
pleship, "follow me" (Mark 1:16) was an imperative to model
one's life on his. Clement of Alexandria expressed it at the end
of the second century: "Our tutor Jesus exemplifies the true
life and trains the one who is in Christ. . . . He gives commands
and embodies the commands that we might be able to accomplish them."[15]

The very existence of the gospels served as a deterrent to the
writing of lives of other holy persons. In them was to be found
the noblest example of all. At this stage of Christian history,
it would have been presumptuous to bring other persons into
competition with the primal model. Only after Nicaea did the
need arise for other exemplars. It should be remembered that
the most potent arrows in the quiver of the Arians were those

passages in the gospels that spoke of Jesus' human features, his limited knowledge, his obedience to God, his growth in wisdom (improvability), his suffering.[16] Once it was declared that the Logos was "of one substance with the Father" (defended chiefly by appeal to the Gospel of John), a vacuum was created that could be filled with other human faces.

Whatever the historical explanation for the rise of Christian hagiography, by the early fourth century Christians began to discover within their midst the human and spiritual resources to embark on a new strategy for teaching virtue. The first intimations of a new way are visible in the relations forged between master and disciple within the Christian community in the second and third centuries. In the ancient world moral education was private and individual, based on a master-disciple relation that was nurtured through bonds of friendship, respect, and admiration; according to Peter Brown, "No student ever went, as we do, to a university conceived of as an impersonal institution of learning. . . . He would always have gone to a person—to Libanius, to Origen, to Proclus."[17] When Gregory the wonderworker came to Caesarea to study with Origen, he wanted, in his words, "to have fellowship with this man" and through him to be transformed. By establishing an intimate personal bond with the student, Origen awakened in him the desire for a new life. The cement of this union was "love," and Gregory says that it was only when he was "smitten" by Origen's love that he was persuaded to give up "those objects that stood in the way of practicing the virtuous life." What goaded the disciple to change was not exhortation but deeds: "He exhorted us by his actions and incited us more by what he did than by what he said."[18]

Gregory did not write a life of Origen, but his "appreciation" of Origen provides a bridge to the first Christian lives. At about the same time that Gregory wrote his essay, Pontus, a disciple of Cyprian, composed what may be considered the first Christian "saint's life." His *Passio et Vita Cypriani*, written shortly after Cyprian's death as a martyr (ca. 259 C.E.), is the work of a man who had served as deacon under the great bishop and knew him well.[19] A more conventional disciple would have written Cyprian's final days in the style of other "acts of the martyrs," a popular literary genre among Christians in North Africa (and elsewhere). Here was a proven form to celebrate the deeds of a holy person in bright and colorful detail. Pontus, however, consciously broke with this tradition. Cyprian, he explained, "had much to teach, *independently* of his martyrdom; what he did *while* he lived should not be hidden from the world." Pontus' purpose in writing the *Vita*, he said, was to hold up the "lofty pattern" *(documentum)* that was displayed in the "actions" and "accomplishments" of Cyprian's entire life, not only his courage at the time of his martyrdom. These deeds, too, were worthy of preservation in "eternal memory."[20]

Although Pontus eschewed the convention of depicting only the final feats of his hero, in one significant respect he stood within the earlier tradition: He wrote about someone he knew at firsthand, not about a hero from the distant past.[21] His life told of a man he loved and admired and who had formed Pontus' own life. The *Vita* summons forth the memories of those who had known Cyprian for years, those who had lived and worked with him, as well as those who had been spectators of his final testimony, his martyrdom.

To a certain extent Pontus' *Vita* was premature. It would be a hundred years before Athanasius wrote the *Life of Antony*. The *Passio et Vita Cypriani*, however, locates a path for us between Christian ethical teaching in the second and third centuries and the works of the fourth and fifth centuries, the great age of Christian hagiography. It foreshadows a development that would alter the face of Christian literature and piety. For with the publication and rapid dissemination of the *Life of Antony*, a new era began. To give but a partial list of the many works that appeared during the next three hundred years testifies to the vitality and breadth of this tradition in the generations after the *Life of Antony: Life of Pachomius*, Palladius' *Life of John Chrysostom*, Gerontius' *Life of Melania* (first full life of a woman ascetic), John Rufus' *Life of Peter the Iberian*, Theodoret of Cyrus' *Religious History*, Cyril of Scythopolis'

Lives of Palestinian Monks, Sulpicius Severus' *Life of Martin of Tours,* John of Ephesus' *Lives of the Eastern Saints.*[22]

Now these works are many and varied. Some are written in an elegant and refined style, self-consciously contraposing Christian saints to the heroes of Greek and Latin antiquity, others are homespun and unaffected tales, ignorant or disdainful of the conventions of the literary culture. Some works dwell on the eccentric and grotesque, men who sat for years on pillars or who lived in huts too narrow to stretch out in; some read like romances and adventure stories; some depict fierce inner struggles; others describe unexceptional acts of mercy or almsgiving; some are frankly apologetic, using the life of the saint to defend a particular theological position (e.g., the christological formulas of Chalcedon) or the view of its critics.

With few exceptions, two features characterize all these lives. First, they hold up "imitation" as the path to virtue. In the *Life of Antony,* Athanasius wrote, "Simply by seeing Antony's conduct many desired to become imitators."[23] Theodoret of Cyrrus, in the preface to his *Religious History* (of the holy men and women of Syria), explained that he was writing down these lives so that others may "imitate" them.[24] The proper subject of the lives are "deeds" not sayings (though they include sayings), i.e., actions that can be emulated or at least admired and venerated. In a letter placed at the beginning of his *Lausiac History,* Palladius wrote: "Words and syllables do not constitute teaching. . . . Teaching consists of virtuous acts of conduct. . . . This is how Jesus taught. . . . He did not use fine language . . . he required the formation of character."[25] As to be expected in works that focus on actions, the lives prize "seeing" over "hearing." The saints are "living icons." A constant refrain is that the author wrote of what he had "seen with his own eyes."[26]

It is only by seeing that one can take the measure of a person's character and remember what one has learned; i.e., to have the saint's character imprinted on one's mind and soul. John of Lycopolis wrote: "We have come to you from Jerusalem for the good of our souls, so that what we have heard with our ears we might perceive with our eyes—for the ears are naturally less reliable than the eyes—and because very often forgetfulness follows what we heard, whereas the memory of what we have seen is not easily erased but remains imprinted on our minds like a picture."[27] As Plutarch recognized, it is sight, visual images formed in the imagination, that have the power to excite in people the desire for emulation.[28]

Second, the subjects of the "lives" are men and women the author knew or about whom reliable information was available from people who knew them. "I write," said Theodoret, about "the glorious saints of our *own* time and the recent past."[29] The lives bear the hues and colors of the communities that produced them. Theodoret calls one of the saints from Cyrus the "fruit of Cyrus."[30] The protagonists are not figures from the past, heroes sanitized by tradition, but gnarly contemporaries. The lives were written as a hedge against forgetfulness of what had taken place in one's midst and in one's "own time." Neither are these tales of kings and generals and seldom do they depict clergy. Most of the heroes are laymen and laywomen. Indeed one of the stock temptations is the lure of ordination, an enticement the best always resist. The lives are stories of simple and unassuming men and women who love God more ardently and serve God more zealously than their neighbors and friends, the kinds of persons who are present in every Christian community, indeed in every religious community.

Of course the lives include stereotypical scenes—the vision of a temptress on the wall of a cave, the wounded lion befriended by the gentle monk, the master gathering his disciples in anticipation of his death—and the portraits are often highly idealized. Yet the fabric of these works bears the imprint of the unique personality of the subject more than the marks of traditional literary conventions or the author's conception of what constitutes a virtuous life. The hagiographers did not offer a grocery list of virtues. The individual life, like the living master, generates its own "criterion for evaluation."[31] The hagiographers wrote about the real accomplishments of living men and women, about deeds that were remembered and admired and evoked to display the saint's unique character, not to illustrate or exemplify a virtue or set of virtues. They filled the space left vacant by the departure of the master.

Once the deeds of virtuous men and women were set within the framework of a life, in contrast to disembodied examples, the possibilities for moral instruction became more subtle and varied.[32] For one thing the hagiographer could exploit the passage of time. No one becomes virtuous in a few weeks or months; holiness is only learned gradually, over a long period of time. True virtue requires years, decades, of guidance, discipline, prayer, and acts of charity. When Sabas, the architect of Palestinian monasticism, comes to Euthymius in the desert east of Jerusalem, he has already excelled in virtue in his homeland Cappadocia; yet when he asks Euthymius, the seer of the Judaean desert, if he can become his disciple, Euthymius says that Sabas is too young (he is eighteen) to adopt the solitary life. He puts him under the care of another monk, Theoctistus, who will lead him in the first steps of monastic discipline. Serving first as muleteer, Sabas gradually takes on whatever other tasks are required. Only after twelve years, when Sabas has reached the age of thirty, is he given permission to live alone, on the condition that he return each week on Saturday and Sunday to the main house. Eventually he is allowed to become a genuine solitary, but it is not until he is forty-five years old that he is entrusted with the direction of other monks.[33]

Spiritual progress is measured not in weeks or months, but in years, even in decades. Twenty, thirty, in some cases, forty years is not uncommon. Saint Antony lives by himself for twenty years "not venturing out and only occasionally being seen by anyone." Only at the end of this time, when his soul has achieved "utter equilibrium," is he ready to accept disciples.[34] Dwelling on the passage of time highlights the value of constancy or steadfastness (in Aristotle's vocabulary, "stability" [bebaiotes]). "Acting in accord with virtue," wrote Aristotle, "must occupy a lifetime. For one swallow does not make spring nor does one fine day summer."[35]

Instead of a single deed there are repeated deeds. Apollonius, a businessman who has renounced the world to live in the Nitrian desert, devotes all his energies to one task. With his own medicine and groceries, he provides for those who are sick: "He could be seen making his round of the monasteries from early morn to the ninth hour, going in door after door to find out if anyone was sick. He used to bring grapes and pomegranates, eggs and cakes such as the sick fancy." This way of life, reported the hagiographer, he practices faithfully and without interruption for *twenty years*.[36]

The lives accentuate habit, the constant performance of good deeds, as the condition for progress in virtue. In modern times no one has expressed this insight more clearly than William James in his *Principles of Psychology*:

> Could the young but realize how soon they will become mere walking bundles of habits, they could give more heed to their conduct while in the plastic state. . . . Every smallest stroke of virtue or vice leaves its never so little scar. The drunken Rip van Winkle, in Jefferson's play, excuses himself for every fresh dereliction by saying, "I won't count this time." Well! He may not count it, and a kind of heaven may not count it; but it is being counted none the less. Down among his nerve-cells and fibres the molecules are counting it, registering and storing it up to be used against him when the second temptation comes. . . . As we become permanent drunkards by so many separate drinks, so we become saints in the moral . . . sphere by so many separate acts.[37]

In contrast to the appeal to stock examples, lives also make a place for the unpredictable and novel. At times it may be nothing more than the playful addition of stray detail to the narrative. Theodore of Sykeon (who spends his time in a cage suspended out over the face of a cliff) is said to have been a swift runner. Several times on a wager he ran a race of three miles with horses and beat them.[38] But more often the unexpected is purposeful, designed to show that the hero is free of the comfortable expectations of society, and enlarges the moral horizon of the hearer.

Marcianos is visited by an older monk, Avitos, who lives in another part of the desert. When Avitos arrives, Marcianos' friend boils some vegetables and greens. After the vegetables have been cooked, Marcianos says to Avitos, "Come my dear friend let us have fellowship together at the table." But Avitos responds: "I don't think I have ever eaten before evening. I often pass two or three days in succession without taking anything." Marcianos (the younger) replies (not without irony), "On my account change your custom today for my body is weak and I am not able to wait until evening." But even that cannot convince Avitos. Marcianos sighs and says, "I am disheartened and my soul is stung because you have expended much effort to come and look at a true ascetic; but instead you are disappointed and behold a tavern keeper and profligate instead of an ascetic." Finally Avitos relents, and Marcianos says: "My dear friend. We both share the same existence and embrace the same way of life, we prefer work to rest, fasting to nourishment, and it is only in the evening that we eat, but we know that love is a much more precious possession than fasting. For the one is the work of divine law, the other of our own power. And it is proper to consider the divine law much more precious than our own." Theodoret, commenting on this virtuous deed, observes that Marcianos knows there is a time for fasting and a time for Christian fellowship. He knows how "to distinguish the different parts of virtue, what can step aside for another, and when to give preference to something else because of the circumstances."[39]

In his *Life of Euthymius*, Cyril of Scythopolis recorded another story with an unexpected ending (in light of what one has already learned about Euthymius). Euthymius is a recluse, and his entire life is marked by a quest for complete solitude (*hesychia*). Yet no matter how deep into the desert he withdraws, people follow him. His life is a story of constant flight to different parts of the Judaean desert, even to the top of Masada (before there was a cable car). His is a stern and uncompromising asceticism, whose chief marks are obedience, fasting, mastery of the passions, solitude. Yet when Euthymius, the great solitary, is about to die, those practices are not the things he speaks of. One year at the feast of Epiphany, a time when Euthymius usually sets off for the "outer desert" to return only at Easter, he does not make his usual preparations. Puzzled, his disciples ask him why. He answers cryptically, "I will remain here this week and on Saturday at night I will leave" (announcing his own death). Three days later he calls his disciples together and addresses them as follows: "My beloved brothers, I go the way of my fathers. If you love me keep these commandments. Hold fast through everything to sincere love which is the beginning and end of all doing of good and the bond of perfection. Just as it is not possible to eat bread without salt, so it is impossible to practice virtue without love. All virtue is established through love and humility by experience and time and grace. Humility, however, exalts ... since the one who humbles himself will be exalted. ... Love is greater than humility."[40]

The *Life of Euthymius* says little of love. Even in the summary of teaching elsewhere in the book, Euthymius does not mention love. According to his biographer, the marks of the monastic vocation are meditation, discernment of spirits, temperance, and obedience.[41] Yet at his death Euthymius speaks only on communal virtues, of the bonds of fellowship, of mutual love.

The lives, then, do not present a single ideal of virtue, nor do they offer one paradigm of holiness. They recognize and recommend different ways of pursuing the goal of perfection, focusing less on traditional virtues than on the unique qualities of a particular person. By displaying how a single person responded to new and varied situations, these stories implicitly suggest that there is no single standard, no one catalogue of virtues, no one way to serve God.

One account deals with two sons of a Spanish merchant. When their father dies, they divide the estate, which consists of five thousand coins, clothes, and slaves, and the sons deliberate on how they should deal with this wealth. Neither wants to be a merchant. Each wants to live a holy life, but they disagree as to what form that should take. So they divide the property and go their separate ways. Paesius gives away everything he has—to the churches, the monasteries, and the prisons—learns a trade to provide for his own needs, and devotes himself to a solitary life of prayer. Isaias keeps the wealth, builds a monastery, takes in some brothers, and welcomes the poor, setting three or four tables on Saturday and Sunday. When the two men die, a dispute arises as to who had chosen the better way. Some claim Paesius excelled because he had hearkened to the command in the gospel to "sell all you have" and follow Jesus (Luke 18:22); others say that Isaias was the greater because he had served others. But Pambo, a wise, old monk, says, "Both are equal." Pambo has had a dream in which he "saw both of them standing in paradise in the presence of God."[42]

Other writers draw an even sharper antithesis between contrasting ways of life. Maesymas is a Syriac-speaking peasant with no education. At first he pursues the solitary life in the desert, but later he comes to live in a village. Unlike the other "ascetic stars" in Theodoret of Cyrus' collection of lives, Maesymas does not sit on a pillar, he does not live in the "open air," he does not weight down his body with chains. He gives himself to the needs of his fellow villagers: "His doors were always open to passers by." Like the widow of Zarephath who fed Elijah, said Theodoret, Maesymas' jar of grain and pitcher of oil are always full. Recognizing that Maesymas does not conform to the conventional picture of a "godly man," Theodoret explained: "Many other stories of this kind are told about this godly person. One can learn from them that those who choose to live virtuously are harmed not at all by life in towns and villages; for this man and those like him responsible for the service of God have shown that it is possible even for those who go about among many to attain the very summit of the virtues."[43] This was quite an admission in an age where the solitary life was the zenith of sanctity.

Theodoret, however, may have felt his praise of Maesymas

to be excessive because he followed his "life" with the tale of one of the true eccentrics: Acepsimas. Theodoret described Acepsimas: "Shutting himself up in a cell, he remained there for sixty years without being seen and without speaking." He has taken to heart the words of the psalm: "Take delight in the Lord." Acepsimas receives food—lentils soaked in water—by stretching his hand through a small hole. Theodoret explained, "To prevent himself from being exposed to those who wished to see him, the hole was not dug straight through the thickness of the wall, but obliquely, being made in the shape of a curve."[44] So holy is Acepsimas that when he dies everyone tries to seize his body and carry it off to his own village. The lives of these holy people do not conform to a predetermined pattern. The saint, like a plant that bends and twists to receive the sun, follows the course of God always turning to the light that is the source of life.

Not only do the lives offer the unexpected—saints who do not always conform to stock virtues or conventional patterns—but they also put a new figure on the stage, the holy woman. There had always been female models—Sarah, Naomi, Judith, Rahab, Mary, Felicity, and Perpetua—but as Christian hagiography matured more and more women became the subjects of lives and their exploits took on new visibility and significance for Christian piety. As has been observed often in recent years, the early Christian monastic movement offered women a way to step free of inherited roles and expectations,[38] and the hagiographers seized the opportunity to tell their stories, some of which are as spellbinding as those of their male counterparts. Melania, for example, is a more extreme ascetic than many men. She wishes to fast even on Easter, she sleeps in sackcloth, and she has a box constructed for sleeping in which she can neither stretch out nor turn over.[45]

What becomes apparent at once in reading the lives of holy women is that they do not cultivate "feminine" virtues. Sylvania, for example, is "erudite and fond of literature" (a kind of patron saint for female seminarians); day and night she reads the ancient Christian commentators, three million lines of Origen and two and a half million lines of Gregory, Basil, and others. She is liberated from "knowledge falsely so called" and is able "to mount on wings . . . and by good hopes she transformed herself into a spiritual bird and so made the journey to Christ."[46] Another woman, Susan, contends with demons. Once she is visited by a "blessed man, great and God-loving" who lives in the desert nearby. Each observes the other in combat with demons. Susan, however, is "stronger than he. She not only conquered the demons, she had no fear of them. She became firm like adamant and unmoveable—so much that the demons would cry out at her, 'This is a woman, but she is stone, and instead of flesh she is iron!'"[47]

The hagiographers' attributions of remarkable feats to women contradicted the popular view that women's capacity for virtue was inferior to that of men. "I must commemorate the courageous women to whom God granted struggles equal to those of men so that no one could plead as an excuse that women are too weak to practice virtue successfully. I have seen a good many of them."[48] Theodoret of Cyrus echoed that idea: "Virtue cannot be separated into male and female. . . . For the difference is one of bodies not of souls," and as the Scripture says, "in Christ Jesus . . . there is neither male nor female. . . . Women too may be models of the virtuous life."[49]

In places the hagiographers allow the reader, though infrequently and exiguously, to glimpse the hero's shortcomings.[50] The saints are not perfect; saints are made, not born. They are impulsive, they backslide, they fall into temptation, they are petty and prideful, they lack self-discipline. A monk at the lavra of Gerasimos in the Jordan valley goes to the abbot and says, "Father, I want to leave the place where I live, because I am very bored."[51] And Conon, a monk in the Jordan valley charged with the responsibility of baptizing, is nonetheless embarrassed and wants to leave the monastery when he has to baptize women. Saint John (the baptizer) appears to Conon and says, "Be patient, I will deliver you from that struggle." Shortly afterward a beautiful Persian maiden comes to be baptized. Conon cannot not baptize her. The bishop, Peter, says that he will

have a deaconess baptize the maiden. Conon, however, wants
to continue in his office. So he goes off by himself for prayer,
and again John the Baptizer appeared to him. "Return," he said,
"to your monastery and I will deliver you from the struggle."
This time Conun replied, "Listen here, I'm not going back.
You've often made promises to me and not kept them." St.
John threw him to the ground, pulled up his habit, marked his
stomach with three crosses, and told him to take courage and go
ahead with the baptism. So Conun returned to the monastery,
baptized the maiden, annointed her with oil, and adds the hagiographer, his body did not move.[52]

The lives, then, do much more than provide a model to imitate. They arouse, judge, inspire, challenge, surprise, amuse,
and excite the reader. Their authors do not simply set down a
minimalist standard for all to imitate. Indeed, many of the specific things they portray are beyond imitation, at least for ordinary mortals. They point beyond the familiar and prosaic to a
higher and more noble vision of the Christian life.[53] One of the
most cited biblical texts was Philippians 3:13: "I forget what
lies behind and strain forward to what lies ahead." What lay
ahead, however, could not be specified for each individual; the
goal was not the same for all. The lives of the saints, in Karl
Jasper's words, serve more as "beacons by which to gain an
orientation" than as "models for imitation."[54] Not everyone
can or will pursue the same path. The criteria for judging virtue
and holiness vary.

The lives of the saints do not present us with a new theory
of virtue, but a new way of teaching virtue, a new strategy that
builds on the tradition of examples, but enriches it by displaying a pattern of holiness over the course of a lifetime.

Precepts are now put in the mouths of familiar persons, and
examples are enhanced by seeing them as deeds of specific individuals. The hagiographers, for the first time in Christian history, turn to living persons, or those who have recently died,
as models of the virtuous life. There is a grest boldness here,
to choose people from one's midst, to hold up to view peasants
and farmers and jugglers and sailors, even bishops, presenting

them as models for their neighbors, fellow citizens, and friends. By displaying men and women from their own time, and often from their own communities, these lives make a proclamation: holiness is possible, virtue is attainable, perfection is within your grasp. They teach, in Bergson's phrase, a morality of aspiration not of obligation.[55] By placing before our eyes deeds that provoke, excite, and charm the ignorant and the educated alike, women and men, city dwellers and farmers, soldiers and kings and merchants, the lives of the saints set us on a sure path toward holiness.

NOTES

1. Origen, *Homilies on Jeremiah*, 4.5.

2. From the passage "Of the Holy Writ in the Life of Father Zossima" in Part One, Book Six, section 2.

3. Plutarch, *Life of Pericles*, 1–4.

4. Seneca, *ep.* 66.

5. Aristotle, *Nichomachean Ethics* 1103b3.

6. On this point see Albrecht Dihle, *Studien zur Griechischen Biographie* (Abhandlungen der Akademie der Wissenschaften in Goettingen, Phil.-hist. Kl, 3 Folge, Nr. 37; Goettingen, 1970), pp. 57–69. On page 57, Dihle writes: "Nur mit Hilfe einer Anzahl in feste, nicht zu komplizierte philosophische Begriffe gefasster Vorstellungen vom Wesen menschlichen Handelns und Lebens, war es moeglich, reihensweise voellig unterschiedlichen Gestalten in ausfuehrlichen, kuensterisch durchgeformten Biographien zu behandeln und dabei nicht nur Ereignisse zu erzaehlen, sondern Personen aus ihrem Leben zu deuten." See also F. Leo, *Die griechische-roemische Biographie nach ihre literarischen Form* (Leipzig, 1901), pp. 104 ff. and Graziano Arrighetti, "Cameleonte, la mimesis e la critica letteraria" in *Poeti, Erudite et Biographi* (Pisa, 1987), pp. 141–59.

7. Plutarch, *Alexander* 1.1–2; see Dihle, *Studien*, p. 62.

8. On "lives in antiquity," see Patricia Cox, *Biography in Late Antiquity*, (Berkeley, 1983); Arnaldo Momigliano, *The Development of Greek Biography* (Cambridge, 1971); A. Dihle, *Studien*; and Dihle's more recent work, *Die Entstehung der historishen Biographie* (Sitzungsberichte der Heidelberger Akademie der Wissenscharten, phil. hist. Klasse, 1986, Bericht 3; Heidelberg, 1987).

9. The Passion of Saint Perpetua and Saint Felicity concludes with these words: "These examples *[exempla]* too should be read aloud for the building up of the church" (21).

10. On the parenetic tradition in early Christianity, see Wayne Meeks, *The Moral World of the First Christians* (Philadelphia, 1988).

11. Col. 3:8; James 1:19, 27.

12. H. Crouzel, "L'Imitation et la 'suite' de Dieu et du Christ dans les premiers siècles chrétiens, ainsi que leur sources gréco-romaines et hébraïques," *Jahrbuch fuer Antike und Christentum* 21 (1978): 7–41.

13. *Wisdom of Sirach*, chapter 44ff. 1 Clement 9; see also 1 Clement 5:1, 16:17; 46:2.

14. See *De Officiis* 1.117; 68; 113; 177. For Ambrose, however, the several virtues are made to fit, willy-nilly, almost any biblical hero.

15. Ignatius of Antioch, Phil. 7:12; Clement of Alexandria, paed. 1.12.98.1–3; also 1 Clement 1:8.

16. On this point, see Robert C. Gregg and Dennis E. Groh, *Early Arianism—A View of Salvation* (Philadelphia, 1981), pp. 1–30.

17. Peter Brown, "The Saint as Examplar in Late Antiquity," in *Saints and Virtues*, ed. John Stratton Hawley (Berkeley, 1987), p. 4.

18. Gregory Thaumaturgus, *Panegyric* 5.70; 6.81; 9.123. For discussion (and bibliography), see Robert L. Wilken, "Alexandria: A School for Training in Virtue," in *Schools of Thought in the Christian Tradition*, ed. Patrick Henry (Philadelphia, 1984), pp. 15–30.

19. The text of *Vita et Passio Cypriani* is edited by A. von Harnack in *Texte und Untersuchungen* 39.3 (Leipzig, 1913).

20. *Vita Cypriani* 1.

21. The author of the Passion of Saint Perpetua and Saint Felicity said that these new displays of virtue *(novae virtutes)* were "not less precious than the examples of old" *(non minora veteribus exempla)* [21]. Contrast, for example, the lives of Abraham or Joseph written by Philo, or Gregory of Nyssa's *Life of Moses*.

22. Many of these "lives" are available in English translations: *The Life of Pachomius*, trans. Apostolos N. Athanassakis (Missoula, 1975); Gerontius, *The Life of Melania the Younger*, trans. Elizabeth A. Clark (New York, 1984); Theodoret of Cyrrhus, *A History of the Monks of Syria* trans. R. M. Price (Kalamazoo, 1985); Sulpicius Severus et al., *The Western Fathers*, trans. F. R. Hoare (1954); Sebastian P. Brock and Susan Ashbrook Harvey, *Holy Women of the Syrian Orient* (Berkeley, 1987); Elizabeth Dawes and Norman H. Baynes, *Three Byzantine Saints* (Crestwood, N.Y. 1977). In the sixth and seventh centuries, there was also a proliferation of portraits of holy persons. See Ernest Kitzinger, "Christian Imagery: Growth and Impact," in *Age of Spirituality: A Symposium*, ed. Kurt Weitzmann (Princeton, 1980), p. 149, and E. Kitzinger, *Late Classical and Mediaeval Studies in Honor of Albert Matthias Friend, Jr.* (Princeton, 1955), pp. 132–50.

23. Athanasius, *Life of Antony* 46. In the introduction, Athanasius wrote, "Since you have asked me about the way of life of the blessed Antony, hoping to learn how he began the discipline, who he was before this, and what sort of death he experienced, and if the things said concerning him are true—so that you also might lead yourselves in *imitation of him*—I received your directive with ready good will."

24. Theodoret of Cyrrhus, *Religious History*, 1–3.

25. Palladius, *The Lausiac History* 1–2, ed. Robert T. Meyer (New York, 1964).

26. Theodoret, *Religious History*, 2, 11; 21.5.

27. John of Lycopolis 19 in *Historia Monachorum*; English translation in *The*

Lives of the Desert Fathers, ed. and trans. Benedicta Ward and Norman Russell (London, 1981), pp. 54–55.

28. In his life of Symeon the Fool, Leontius, bishop of Neapolis in Cyprus wrote: "For those who are zealously devoted in soul to God, *conscience* is a sufficient basis for teaching. It exhorts us to do good things and diverts us from evil things. To those who are more humble than these, there is need of the *precepts* of the law and exhortation. If, however, someone slips through the first or second way which leads to virtue, such a one can only be aroused to desire God . . . and to pursue the hard and difficult way, by the zeal and devotion of those who he lives he sees or about whom he hears a story" (*Patrologia Graeca* 93. 1669–71).

29. Theodoret, *Religious History*, 1.1.

30. *Ibid.*, 17.2.

31. The phrase is from A. S. Cua, *Dimensions of Moral Creativity: Paradigms, Principles and Ideals* (University Park, 1978), 40.

32. In defending her preference for "tragedies" over "examples" to illuminate moral action, Martha Nussbaum (in *The Fragility of Goodness, Luck and Ethics in Greek Tragedy and Philosophy* [Cambridge, 1986], p. 14) writes: "We can say provisionally that a whole tragic drama, unlike a schematic philosophical example making use of a similar story, is capable of tracing the history of a complex pattern of deliberation, showing its roots in a way of life and looking forward to its consequences in that life. As it does all of this, it lays open to view the complexity, the indeterminacy, the sheer difficulty of actual human deliberation. If a philosopher were to use Antigone's story as a philosophical example, he or she would, in setting it out schematically, signal to the reader's attention everything that the reader ought to notice. He would point out what is strictly relevant. A tragedy does not display the dilemmas of its characters as pre-articulated; it shows them searching for the morally salient; and it forces us, as interpreters, to be similarly active. Interpreting a tragedy is a messier, less determinate, more mysterious matter than assessing a philosophical example; and even when the work has once been interpreted, it remains unexhausted, subject to reassessment, in a way that the example does not."

33. Cyril of Scythopolis, *Life of Sabas*, ed. Eduard Schwartz, *Texte und Untersuchungen* 49 (Leipzig, 1939); French translation by A. J. Festugiere, *Les Moines d'Orient* 3.2 (Paris, 1962).

34. Athanasius, *Life of Antony* 14, trans. Robert Gregg (New York, 1980), p. 42.

35. Aristotle, *Nichomachean Ethics* 1098 a115–16.

36. Palladius, *Lausiac History* 13; pp. 48–49.

37. William James, *The Principles of Psychology* (New York, 1910), p. 127.

38. *Life of Theodore of Sykeon* 13; trans. Elizabeth Dawes and Norman H. Baynes (Crestwood, N.Y., 1977), p. 13.

39. Theodoret, *Religious History* 3.12.

40. Cyril of Scythopolis, *Life of Euthymius* 39; French translation by A. J. Festugiere in *Les Moines d'Orient* 3.1 (Paris, 1962).

41. Cyril of Scythopolis, *Life of Euthymius* 9.

42. Palladius, *Lausiac History* 14. Other stories make a similar point. The anchorite Paphnutius, after hearing of the good deeds of a practitioner of the despised occupation of flute playing, said, "I am not aware myself of having accomplished anything equal to this." (John of Lycopolis, *Historia Monachorum* 14; see Ward and Russell translation, p. 95.)

43. Theodoret, *Religious History* 14.

44. Theodoret, *Religious History* 15.

45. *Life of Melania* 25, 31, 32. Before she gave birth to her son (stillborn), she spent the night in the chapel kneeling and keeping vigil (5). The Latin version of the life says that Melania's father sent eunuchs to make certain she was in her room sleeping. Melania bribed them so they would not tell her father where she was (Elizabeth A. Clark, *Ascetic Piety and Women's Faith: Essays on Late Ancient Christianity* [New York, 1986], p. 189, n. 6.)

46. Palladius, *Lausiac History* 41.

49. Theodoret, *Religious History* 30. Theodoret of Cyrus cites Gal. 3:28: "There is neither Jew nor Greek, there is neither slave nor free, there is neither male nor female." A similar point is made by John of Ephesus in his lives of Mary and Euphemia: "Since we learn from the divine Paul who said, 'In Christ Jesus there is neither male nor female,' it seemed to us that we should introduce the story of those who are by nature females, since mention of them in no way lessens this series of stories about holy men. Furthermore, their course of life was not lower than the exalted path upon which every one of these holy men has journeyed, and even their way of life was great and surpasses telling" (*Holy Women of the Syrian Orient*, p. 124).

50. Shortcomings are revealed only up to a point. The hagiographers are chary of criticizing their heroes. By contrast, Jews felt no such constraints. An instructive case is the difference in the portrait of Joseph by Christians (e.g., Ambrose's *De Josepho*) and that by Jews (e.g., in *Genesis Rabbah* 84.51). I am indebted for this point to a seminar paper by Margaret Mohrmann, "The Patriarch Joseph: Chaste Perfection or Vain Ambition: His Portraits in Early Christian and Jewish Literature" (University of Virginia, Fall, 1988). For a discussion of why "sainthood" has played a minor role in Judaism, see Robert L. Cohn, "Sainthood on the Periphery: The Case of Judaism," in *Saints and Virtues*, pp. 87–110.

51. John Moschus, *Pratrum Spirituale*, 142.

52. *Ibid.*, 3.

53. Iris Murdoch writes: "In assessing people we do not consider only response to particular problems, but look for their total vision as shown in their mode of speech or silence, their choice of words, their assessments of others, their conceptions of their own lives, what they think attractive or praiseworthy . . . in short, the configurations of their thought which show continually in their reactions and conversations" ("Vision and Choice in Morality," in Paul Ramsey, ed., *Christian Ethics and Contemporary Philosophy* [New York, 1966], p. 202).

54. Karl Jaspers, *Socrates, Buddha, Confucius, and Jesus: The Four Paradigmatic Individuals* (New York, 1957), p. 96.

55. Henri Bergson, *Two Sources of Morality* (New York, 1935), p. 43. See also Kai Nielsen, "Why Should I Be Moral," in Paul Taylor, ed., *Problem of Moral Philosophy* (1967), p. 516: Nielson states, "For the most part, people get their standards not from ethical treatises or even scriptural texts or homely sayings, but by idealizing and following the example of some living person or persons."

Christology in the
Jewish-Christian Dialogue

JÜRGEN MOLTMANN

LET ME BEGIN with a few introductory remarks about Christian-Jewish dialogue: I believe the truth is dialogical. Only in dialogue can we discover the truth because only in relationship to others do we form our own identity. We need the eyes of others to understand ourselves. When encountering another person and hearing the words "I see you," and "I know you," we begin to see ourselves and to understand ourselves. Otherwise, we would sit incarcerated in our prejudices and our anxieties. One does not lose one's authentic identity in dialogue with others but rather one gains a new profile over against the other. To enter, however, into a dialogue with Jews is for Christians, especially Christians in Germany, a humbling process, full of pain and shame, for to recognize ourselves in the eyes of Jews means to be looked upon by the eyes of the victims and the survivors of Auschwitz. Yet, for Christians, it is the only way to recognize the actual history, and also, to authentic Christian existence "after Auschwitz." Clearly, one does not invite the victims to dialogue, but the dialogue, which Jews have begun with us Christians in Germany after the Second World War, is a precious offer. It was and still is an offer, which has again given hope to many of us in our despair under long shadows of Auschwitz. In this dialogue we discover that the Christian tradition has formulated Christology, the central point of theology, from the beginning often in an anti-Judaistic, and not in a pro-Judaistic, form. The Jewish-Christian dialogue today inspires us to revise and reformulate Christology.

77

There is no Christology without presuppositions. The presupposition of Christology is the messianic promise of the Scripture and the hope of the present Israel. Only when one sees Jesus and his history in light of the promises of the Scripture and of Israel's history of hope, does one truly understand him. What does "Christology" mean other than messianology? The Christ is the Messiah of Israel.

The "Christian" messianology is certainly characterized by the unique historical figure of Jesus of Nazareth and his special history. Nevertheless, the Scriptures and the history of Israel, in which Jesus lived and out of which he gained his theological meaning as the Christ, must be continually remembered. Therefore, we will not understand "Christ" as a proper name, as it already was done in the early Hellenistic communities, but rather as his function for the people and for the coming God. Instead, we have to again and again retranslate the Christ title back into the Messiah title and take up its original meanings: Jesus = the Messiah; the church = the messianic community; being a Christian = a human existence in hope. "Christian" is not a party name, but rather a promise: the messianic. In this essay, we ask first about the category of the "messianic" in order to develop the fundamental technological category for the specific Christology of Jesus. The term *messianic* is to encompass the Messiah in person as well as the messianic kingdom, the messianic time as well as the messianic land, the messianic signs, and the messianic days in history. The term *messianic* is certainly developed from the person and the history of Jesus. What else could a "heathen Christian" do? But the term should be developed in such an open way that it respects the Jewish messianic hope and is unfolded in constant dialogue with Jewish philosophers of religion.

The Christian Christology divides Christians and Jews. But it must not deteriorate into an anti-Jewish theology because it is the messianic hope that also connects Christians and Jews. Therefore, no Christian Christology may attempt to liquidate the Jewish messianic hope: Jesus is not "the end of the Messiah." And therefore no Christian Christology is allowed to want to inherit the Jewish messianic hope in order to consciously or unconsciously declare the previous owner to be dead: Jesus is not the terminal "fulfillment" of the messianic hope.

The Christian Christology is a certain form of Israel's messianic hope, and it remains related to and dependent on the Jewish forms of the messianic hope before it and beside it. "Messianism is the most original idea of Judaism," claimed Martin Buber rightfully.[1] "Messianism is the idea, which Israel gave to the world," conceded Gershom Scholem.[2] It is the Scriptures in their entirety that, as the "book of a constantly growing expectation" (according to G. v. Rad), points beyond itself and every historical fulfillment into the future of the "coming one." In the prophetic interpretation of the history of Israel, an "explosive" accumulated, but when "the explosion comes," said Buber, "it is not the revolutionary, but the messianic."[3] Christianity can be perceived as a way in which Israel permeates the world with messianic hope for the coming God. Christianity loses nothing when it acknowledges this lasting Jewish root of its hope. Judaism does not compromise itself in any way when it acknowledges the "mysterious," as Martin Buber expressed it; that is, promulgation of the name, the commandment, and the kingdom of God through Christianity, as the great Maimonides did in the Middle Ages, when he understood this phenomenon of Christianity as "praeparatio messianica" of the people of the world for the world-wide coming of the kingdom of Israel's God. We will try to develop a Christology on the basis of this common messianism and of a Jewish-Christian dialogue.

Categories of the Messianic

The phenomena of the Old Testament, the Jewish and the Christian messianism are so colorful and ambiguous that it is impossible to construe a theological system out of the messianism.[4] But because these phenomena play a central role in the legacy of the Scriptures, it is reasonable to investigate essential categories of the messianic.

Gershom Scholem and Walter Benjamin have pointed out the extraordinary experience of the historical breach of the year A.D. 587, the destruction of Jerusalem and the end of political independence of Israel, out of which the messianic idea is born and at which it, in turn, is aimed. Scholem writes, "The Jewish messianism is in its origin and essence, and this cannot be overemphasized, a catastrophe theory. This theory emphasizes the subversive, revolutionary element in the transition from each historical presence to the messianic future."[5] Here Scholem combines, however, two different subversions: first, the decline and then, the transition. The first subversion is a catastrophe; the second, the rescue. Both are leaps as Scholem indicates: transitionless transitions. In Scholem's work the leap into the messianic future presupposes the fall into the misery of the historical present. Let us go back to the origin of Israel's messianic hope. It has not been born simply out of a historical disappointment, as Buber interprets psychologically, but concretely out of the overwhelming of Israel through the superpower Babylon, the subjection of the people and their enslavement. This is stressed by all commentators of the great prophecy in Israel. Gerhard von Rad has stressed this theopolitical experience of the break of the traditions and institutions on which Israel had been based up to then. Therefore, he put his "theology of the prophetic traditions of Israel" under the heading from Isaiah 43:18: "Remember not the former things nor consider the things of old. Behold, I am doing a new thing." The break of the old is the presupposition of the new and the prophetic new "is—the controversial term can not be avoided—the eschatological."[6] It is—in my terminology—the messianic in the eschatological. The theological-political break of the old is a catastrophe.

The catastrophe makes old what has so far been the enduring basis and distinguishes the times of history in a "before" and an "after" so clearly that past and future cannot appear on one and the same time continuum. They have become two different ages. After the catastrophe the people have, in a certain way, arrived at the zero point. There is the danger that they will dissolve and pay homage to the gods of the stronger ones because their own catastrophe is also the catastrophe of their trust in God and with that, the catastrophe of their God as well. Can one still be "Israel" after such a catastrophe? Apparently, the people have not seen themselves placed in front of this choice. Because of their election by God, they did not have this choice. The election consciousness must have been so strong that it maintained the identity of the people. This was the hour of the prophets and the hour of birth of the messianic hope. Having perished in the catastrophe, the old traditions become future-oriented memories by virtue of the hope for the new beginning that the electing God will set for the people through his Messiah-King. One can, of course, judge this as an "idealization" of the time that was irrevocably gone. But before such judgment, it is a normal cognitive process: Only abroad does one know how to value one's home. Only when we are driven out of the Paradise, do we know what the Paradise is. Each recognition needs distance and alienation. In the midst of things, one is blind to them. For that reason only the prophetic messianic hope makes clear what history has to say about the anointed One of Yahweh and about David. The hope of the new Jerusalem actualizes what the old Jerusalem in truth has been.

History understood as continuum, development, and progress can only be the history of the conquerors, who develop their power. The historical experience of the conquered, subjected, and enslaved is the experience of discontinuity and longing for a new start, the suffering from decline, and the hope to rise again. The suffered catastrophe allows for nothing but the hope that the circumstances that have come about will be overthrown. One can identify this concept as the "revolutionary element" in the messianic hope.

The question "When does the Messiah come?" will not be answered on the linear time line, but through the qualification of the situation (kairos), which makes his entrance possible and necessary. The conditions for his coming are mentioned, but the date is not named: "The Messiah comes, when all the guests are seated at the table"; "The Messiah comes, when all of Israel celebrates one Sabbath or when all of Israel celebrates no Sabbath"; and "The Messiah comes like a thief in the night." The "transitionless transition" into the time of the Messiah is as unpredictable as a miracle or a leap into another quality of the history. "Three things come inadvertently: the Messiah, a discovery, a scorpion," wrote a Talmud teacher in the third century.[7] From this result come two possibilities:

1. The Messiah comes when he becomes necessary. When the distress is the worst and one has given up all hope, then he comes. Because the messianic redemption answers the historical catastrophe, this catastrophe theory, which has to be called apocalyptic, is based on good reasons. It deprives the Messiah of the freedom to come, however, when he considers it right to come and it blackmails him, so to speak, with the opposite. When the world falls and is thrown into the catastrophe, then the redemption comes as its contrary. This apocalyptic catastrophe thinking also appears in the modern nuclear age. But it is a wrong calculation and nothing but the justification of the crime of the nuclear inferno.

2. The Messiah comes, when it becomes possible, because the way has been prepared for him. This is the advice of the prophets (Isa. 40): Prepare the way of the Lord! Repent! Become light! Lift your heads! The Messiah does not come unannounced. He has his Gospel, through which he announces himself; it precedes his coming. In this sense Buber may be right: "All of time is directly related to redemption, all action for God's sake may be called messianic action."[8] This quotation does not mean that human acts of goodness bring the messianic redemption closer or that it even is the messianic redemption itself. It does mean, however, that the hope for the coming of the Messiah already becomes active here and now in a messianic way. This is the "improvement of the world for the Kingdom of God," as it is called in the Jewish Alenu prayer. "To mend the world" by bringing a tikkun into the world, an improvement there, where the world has become fragile.[9] The tikkun is of course more than a repair of the world because the completion of tikkun is the Kingdom of the Messiah and in its

way, the Kingdom of God himself. As each *tikkun* realizes an objective possibility, the splinters of the messianic time must be interspersed with the historical time of the present. Each moment can become a messianic moment in this sense; "each second the little gate, through which the Messiah" can step.[10] To prepare the way for the Messiah means to live in the light of Advent and to open oneself together with this world for the coming One. It means to anticipate his coming in recognition and action and to make visible with all strength and as much as possible some part of that redemption of all things "already now," which the Messiah will complete in his days. Does this mean to "press" for the end and to "force" the Messiah into coming? "Certainly the seduction to action, the call for accomplishment"[11] is part of the Jewish messianism in its utopian element, as Gershom Scholem says. The Christian messianism also knows the uprising of eschatological impatience for the realization of what is hoped for. These are not only the millenialist and revolutionary movements of the Taborites, Anabaptists, and Puritans. The difference between forcing the Messiah by deepening the catastrophe and by anticipating his kingdom oneself is not so deep as Scholem thinks. Apocalyptics and revolutionaries come from the same family. Between them runs the line of the patient compassion for the messianic action, the acting hope, the expectant liberation of the poor and oppressed, the messianic *tikkun* ethics.

Scholem has vividly described the big danger of the messianic thinking and life as the "price of messianism." "To live in the hope is something great, but it is also something deeply unreal . . . in Judaism the messianic idea has imposed the *life in deferment,* in which nothing can be done and complete in a final manner."[12] Messianic hope can indeed work in both directions: It can draw the heart of the human out of the present and set it into the future: "Next year in Jerusalem." Then the messianic hope depletes the present life, the action, but naturally also the suffering from the present oppressions. But it can also actualize the future of the Messiah and fill the present with the consolation and the happiness of the closeness of God. Then the messianic idea does not impose a *"life in deferment"* but rather a *life in anticipation* in which everything must be done and completed in final form because the Messiah has already come near.

What Scholem leaves unmentioned is the situation of the people who live with the messianic hope because they have survived with this hope. To the "people, who live in darkness," the slaves, prisoners, exploited and oppressed, this hope is not something "unreal" but their present reality. If they have life and human dignity, then it is in and from the hope. The messianic hope for a future that will change everything is what makes the prisoners not put up with the prison and the slaves not bow to their owners. The messianic hope makes them live in an "upright way" despite their present reality. If this hope did not exist, then one would resign oneself to this situation of slowly dying. One would "bend down so low 'till down don't bother you no more." That one does not resign but that one feels the injustice in the pain and rebels against it is due to the inextinguishable hope.

3. There is an unequivocal anticipation of the messianic time in the middle of historical time, which is the Sabbath. The weekly Sabbath actualizes the festival of the creation in the "quiet of God," in which humans and animals are to come to rest. But at the same time, it also anticipates the messianic time. The songs of the "third meal" on the Sabbath afternoon "are full of the ecstasy of the certainly nearing future of the Messiah."[13] In the presence of the Sabbath, the festival of the creation, the festival of liberation and the festival of redemption is celebrated. In respect to the redemption, the Sabbath can be called "a sixtieth of the coming world."[14] As it represents the anticipatory start of the messianic time, the coming messianic time is imagined as the "Sabbath without end." It is said, "When all of Israel celebrates a Sabbath, the Messiah comes." This means the common and real celebration of Sabbath is the messianic time and vice versa. But this also means that in each real Sabbath celebration the Messiah enters through this door into the present and comes in together with "Queen Sabbath."

The Sabbath day of the week points beyond itself to the Sabbath year. The Sabbath year points beyond itself to the Year of Jubilee and the Year of Jubilee points to the Sabbath of the messianic time and the Sabbath of the messianic time points to the eternal Sabbath of God. The Sabbath day is a kind of messianic intermezzo in the historical time; the Sabbath celebration, a kind of messianic sacrament of time. Through the regular Sabbath days and Sabbath years, the Coming One makes time move, so to speak, in the messianic rhythm of his expectation. There is no continuum between the Sabbath and the time of work. Rather the Sabbath interrupts the time of work because people come to rest and nature is allowed to come to rest. The Sabbath thereby opens both for the arrival of the totally other time of the Messiah. The Sabbath makes them ready for the arrival of the Messiah in the midst of transitoriness. Compared to the noisy messianism of the catastrophe-apocalypticism and the excited messianism of the revolutionary utopianism, the Sabbath is a quiet but persistent and therefore, long-term messianism. It comes in the daily life and brings the dream of the redemption into the insignificant of the lived life.

Christology in the Jewish-Christian Dialogue

In the center of all Jewish-Christian conversations inevitably stands the Messiah question: "Are you he who is to come, or shall we look for another?" The Messiah hope leads us to Jesus, but it also prevents Jews from seeing in Jesus of Nazareth the expected Messiah, who has already come. Jesus answers the messianic questions by his proclamation of the kingdom to the poor and his signs and miracles. The gospels integrate his entire appearance in the horizon of the messianic hope, which obviously makes it impossible for "all of Israel" to have already understood Jesus as the Messiah. Because the early Christian Christology originated in this tension, each Christian Christology must come back to the conflict and come to terms with the Jewish no.[15] It is the fundamental question in the center of Christian Christology: Is the Jewish no anti-Christian? Is the

Christian yes anti-Jewish? Are the no or yes of these questions final or temporary, are they exclusive, or can they also gain dialectical positive meaning for those who must say it?

The Jewish No

In his dialogue with the New Testament scholar Karl-Ludwig Schmidt on January 14, 1933, in the Jewish School (Lehrhaus) in Stuttgart, Martin Buber formulated the protest against the Messiahship of Jesus in such a classic manner that since then, it has always been repeated by Jews: "The Church is based on the belief that Christ has come as the redemption, which humanity has been granted by God. We of Israel are not *capable* of believing this." The question is not about resentment or a stubborn reaction of defiance, but a "not-being-able-to-accept." With the high respect that Buber had for Jesus and also for Christianity, there is a deeper experience, which makes him confess this incapacity:

> More deeply, more truly we know that world history has not been broken open in its very basis, that the world is not yet redeemed. We feel the non-redemption of the world. As for this feeling of ours, the Church can or must understand it as the consciousness of *our* non-redemption. But we know differently. For us, the redemption of the world is inseparably one with the completion of the creation with the establishment of the unity, which is not hindered by anything anymore, which does not suffer from any contradiction, but is realized in all the variety in the world. Redemption of the world is one with the fulfillment of the Kingdom of God. An anticipation of the redemption of the world as already completed in some part, for instance, that the soul would already be redeemed, we are not able to grasp even though redeeming and being redeemed also make themselves known to us in our mortal hours. We do not perceive a caesura in history. We know no middle in it, but only a goal, the goal of the way of God, who does not stop on his way.[16]

Scholem Ben-Chorin took up this argument early on:

> The Jew deeply knows about this non-redemption of the world and he knows and acknowledges no enclaves of redemption in the middle of this non-redemption. The idea of the redeemed soul in the middle

of a non-redeemed world is foreign to him, foreign in its very basis, inaccessible from the basis of his existence. Here lies the core for the rejection of Jesus by Israel, not in an only-external, only-national idea of Messianism. Redemption means in the eyes of a Jew, redemption from all evil. Evil of the body and the soul, evil of the creation and of the culture. Therefore when we say redemption, we mean the entire redemption. We know only one caesura between creation and redemption, the revelation of God's will.[17]

Can there then be *anticipations* or *anticipatory starts* of the redemption before the final, total, and universal redemption of the world? Can the Redeemer himself already be in the world before the redemption of the world? Can one already be a Christian in this unredeemed world and exist as a person of messianic hope? Before we attempt to answer this critical questioning of the Christian existence, we must turn the question around because the argument with the "un-redeemed world" also falls back onto the Jewish existence. As a "heathen Christian," one must therefore also ask Israel this "heathen question": Can there be a chosen people of God already before the redemption of the world? Does not the election of Israel destroy Israel's solidarity with the non-redeemed people? And if this world is so totally non-redeemed, is then not the Jewish caesura, the revelation of the will of God on Sinai and a God-obedient life in the middle of all of this evil an impossible possibility, asking too much for Israel?

Simply asked, can one already be a Jew in this godless world? Is not Israel, the "people of choice" and the "people of God's will," something completely unique in the world of humans? In light of the messianic hoped-for-redemption of the world, one will be thankful for the miracle of the prophetic existence of Israel. Because if there were no anticipatory appearance of the redemption in this world, why should one actually consider the world as non-redeemed? The hard fact of the "non-redeemed world" is not only evidence against the Christians but also against the Jews inasmuch as both in their respective ways of hoping contradict the non-redeemed world and resist its evils.

The picture that Buber, Ben-Chorin, and Scholem draw of Christianity is true for a certain historical Christianity. But it is not true for Jesus himself and also not essentially true for the authentic Christian confession of him. These writers only question the allegedly "Christian" conception of redemption, not the Christian existence.

The Christian Yes

The Messiah, who has come in Jesus of Nazareth, is the suffering servant of God who heals through his wounds and wins through his suffering. He is not yet the Parousia-Christ, who comes in the glory of God and redeems the world to the kingdom. What has come through the coming and presence of Christ in the world is already the justification of the godless and the reconciliation of the enemies, but not yet the "redemption of the world." The grace of God has been revealed through Christ. But the glory of God has not broken through its secrecy yet. Exactly because we "already now" have peace with God through Christ, we are "no longer" resigned to this world without peace. Because we are reconciled with God, we suffer from this "nonredeemed world" and "sigh" together with all of the enslaved creation (Rom. 8).

Also the resurrected Christ himself is "not yet" the Pantocrator. But he is on the way to the redemption of the world. The *Christian yes* to Jesus' messiahship based on believed and experienced reconciliation will therefore acknowledge the *Jewish no* based on experienced and suffered non-redemption of the world and will respect this no in that it speaks of that total and universal world redemption only in the dimensions of future hope and of the present contradiction to this nonredeemed world. The *Christian yes* to Jesus the Christ is also not completed and finished within itself but open in itself for the future of Jesus Christ. It is an eschatological anticipatory and *preliminary yes:* "Amen. Yes, come, Lord Jesus!" (Rev. 22:20). Therefore, the Christian yes cannot be an exclusive nor excommunicating yes, not when it is spoken with the certainty of confession. Whoever confesses Jesus as the "Christ of God" recognizes Christ as becoming—the Christ on the way, the Christ in the movement of the eschatological history of God— and steps into the following of Jesus on this "way of Christ."[18] The earthly Jesus was on the way to the revelation of his Messiahship. This is called the "Messianic secret" of Jesus. The resurrected Lord is on the way to his rule—which only begins here, but is still not universal in any way—in order to hand over at the end the completed rule to God, who then will be "everything to everyone" (1 Cor. 15:28) and comes to his immediate kingdom.

> The earthly → the crucified → the resurrected → the present → the coming One

These are the stations of the eschatological history of God with Jesus, which the Christ title is to name and the Christology is to comprehend and permeate spiritually. We can apply here an old distinction of theology: There is here and now a theologia viae; there will be a theologia patriae in heaven. Analogously, we have here and now a Christologia viae and a Christologia patriae then: the Parousia of Christ. This distinction excludes every triumphalism from Christology. Jesus "the Lord," as the early community confessed him, is on the way to his rule not only through the coming times but also through the spaces. He goes the way from Israel to the people and from the people to Israel again. The way of Christ exists under the feet of those who take it. To take the "way of Christ" means to believe in him. To believe in him means to go with him on his present path. "I am the way" is an old Johannine predication of Jesus (John 14:6).

God's Yes in the Jewish No

When the *Jewish no* to the Messiahship of Jesus is not based on resentment or bad will but on an "incapacity," as Buber says, then there is no reason for Christians to deplore this no or to make a rebuke out of it. The no of Israel is not identical to the no of the nonbelievers, who are everywhere. It is a special no and must be respected as such.

In the Israel chapter of Romans 9–11, Paul saw Israel's no as the will of God. Israel is "hardened," not because it says no; rather it can do nothing but say no because it is "hardened" by God. To be "hardened" is not to be rejected. It is a historical, not a final, act of God. It is an act for a definite purpose, as the Moses-Pharaoh story shows. To what purpose does God burden all of Israel with the incapacity for the yes of the faith in Jesus? The purpose is that the Gospel passes on from Israel to the Gentiles and "the last" become the first. Without the Jewish no, the Christian Church would have remained an inner-Jewish, messianic revival movement. But together with the Jewish no, the Christian community made the surprising discovery that the Spirit comes to Gentiles so that Gentiles are directly led to Christian faith without previously becoming Jewish. The mission to the nations, which Paul himself began, is a direct fruit of the Jewish no. He also made this very clear to the Christian community in Rome, which consisted of Jews and Gentiles. Paul writes, "As regards the gospel they are enemies of God, for your sake; but as regards election they are beloved for the sake of their forefathers" (Rom. 11:28). One can therefore rightly say, "We will only have left the Christian anti-Judaism behind us, when we theologically succeed in finding something positive in the Jewish no to Jesus Christ."[19] This "positive" lies in the mission to the nations, out of which the Church arises. It is not only something positive that one makes out of the negative but it is, according to Paul, the will of God, which has become revealed in the Jewish resentment of the gospel. Therefore, the Jewish Christian Paul can indeed deplore the Jewish no and mourn for his own people (Rom. 9:2–5), but at the same time also praise the yes of God, which is revealed out of this no: "Their failure means riches for the Gentiles" (Rom. 11:12) and "their rejection means the reconciliation of the world" (Rom. 11:15).

By no means can it be said that God has finally rejected the people of his choice—then he would have to reject his own choice (Rom. 11:29)—and has sought a new people for himself with the Church. The promises of Israel have not passed on to the Church; the Church does not oust Israel from her place in the history of God. In the perspective of the Gospel, Israel has in no way become like all other people. And finally, with its no, Israel is also not a historical witness for the judgment of God and not only a warning for the community of Christ. Exactly because the Gospel has come to the people because of the Jewish no, it will return to Israel. The "first will be the last." Everything runs in its direction. For Paul, this was an apocalyptic "mystery": "a hardening has come upon part of Israel, until the full number of the Gentiles come in, and so all Israel will be saved; as it is written, 'The Deliverer will come from Zion, he will banish ungodliness from Jacob'" (Rom. 11:25–26). This "Redeemer" of Israel for Paul, the Christ of the Parousia, the Messiah, comes in the glory of God and his name is Jesus. The Jewish no, which Saul embodied with particular fervor against the early Christian communities, was overcome through a vocational vision of the crucified one in the glory of God. Therefore, Paul directs his hope for his people to the Redeemer, who comes in glory "from Zion." He expects from the Redeemer no conversion of the Jews or their coming to the Christian faith but rather Israel's redemption and resurrection from the dead: "What will their acceptance mean, but life from the dead?" (Rom. 11:15). The redemption in glory happens not only to the last surviving generation but across the times of history to all dead together "in one moment." The redemption hope of the Apostle refers to all of Israel in all times. His practical answer to the Jewish no is not an anti-Judaism but the evangelization of the nations. For him, this evangelization also brings the day of redemption closer to Israel.

If the Christian yes, which in the Jewish no discovers the positive and the will of God, is to be sought for in this direction, then this is also the approach to a "Christian theology of Judaism" or to a Christology, which is not anti- but pro-Judaistic. But this is only possible for Christian theology when Jewish theology tries to understand the mystery of Christianity on the basis of Jewish no. It is indeed an unreasonable demand "after Auschwitz," but it must also be a theological question for faithful Jews: What will of God expresses itself in the mission and propagation of Christianity? Through the mission of the Gospel, the name of the Lord is made known to the ends of the earth and the Christian world daily prays together with Israel for the consecration of the name, the doing of the will, and the coming of the Kingdom of God! Can Israel not see, even with all respect for the Jewish no, Christianity as the *praeparatio messianica* of the nations, like Maimonides did, and with that, recognize the way of its own messianic hope in Christianity?[20]

Would not the messianic preparation of the nations for the coming of the redemption be without basis if it did not come from the Messiah himself? From his future he comes through his Gospel into the present and opens the people through hope for the redemption of this non-redeemed world.

NOTES

1. Martin Buber, *Werke* 2 (Munich, 1964), 41.

2. Gershom Scholem, "Zum Verständnis der messianischen Idee," *Judaica* 1 (Frankfurt, 1963), 73.

3. Buber, *Werke* 2:388; R. R. Geis, *Von unbekannten Judentum* (Freiburg, 1961), 158f.

4. Originally Ernst Bloch wanted to draw up a "system of theoretical messianism," but what arose was *The Spirit of Utopia* (1918, 1923).

5. Scholem, art. cit., 20; Walter Benjamin, "Geschichtsphilosophische Thesen VII," in *Illuminationen: Ausgewählte Schriften* (Frankfurt, 1961), 227f., 280.

6. Gerhard von Rad, *Theologie des Alten Testaments* 2 (Munich, 1960), 127.

7. Cited by Scholem, art. cit., 26.

8. Buber, *Werke* 4:756.

9. Emil Fackenheim, "To Mend the World," in *Foundations of Future Jewish Thought* (New York, 1982), esp. 250ff.

10. Benjamin, art. cit., 279.

11. Scholem, art. cit., 34.

12. Ibid., 73f.

13. Franz Rosenzweig, *Der Stern der Erlösung*, 3rd ed. (Heidelberg, 1954), 3:67.

14. Berachot 57 b.

15. Cf. Jacob Petuchowski and Jürgen Moltmann, "Die messianische Hoffnung," *Conc*(D) 10 (1974) 589–91, 592–96.

16. Buber, *Werke* 4:562.

17. Schalom Ben-Chorin, *Die Antwort des Jona: Zum Gestaltwandel Israels* (Hamburg 1956), 99, with reference to his *Die Christusfrage an die Juden* (Jerusalem, 1941), 25.

18. See also Rosemary Ruether ("In What Sense Can We Say That Jesus Was 'The Christ'?" *The Ecumenist* 10 [1972] 22), for whom Jesus will only be the Christ in the fullest sense of the word at the end of time. Jesus is the Christ now in the sense that he has anticipated the divine victory at the end. Because she has taken the basic ideas of an eschatological theology from the *Theology of Hope,* I agree with her against her critics. See my *Theology of Hope,* 87: "Jesus reveals and identifies himself as the Lord on the way to his coming lordship, and to that extent in differentiation from the one he will be" (ET slightly altered).

19. Fr.-W. Marquardt, "Feinde um unsretwillem: Das judische Nein und die christliche Theologie" (1977), in *Verwegenheiten: Theologische Stücke aus Berlin* (Munich, 1981), 311.

20. See J. Klausner, *Jesus von Nazarethi Sein Leben und seine Lehre,* 2nd ed. (Jerusalem, 1952; ET *Jesus of Nazareth: His Life, Times and Teaching,* trans. from Hebrew by J. Danby [London and New York, 1925]), 572: "From a general human point of view he is certainly 'a light to the Gentiles'. His disciples carried Israel's teaching to the Gentiles in all parts of the world, even if in mutilated and incomplete form. In this sense, no Jew can deny the importance of Jesus and his teaching for the history of the world. And in fact neither Maimonides nor Jehuda Halevi failed to recognize this aspect" (translated from the German text). Schalom Ben Chorin goes a step further; see "Did God Make Anything Happen in Christianity? An Attempt at a Jewish Theology of Christianity," *Christian Identity: Concilium* 192, no. 2 (1988) 61–70. He seeks for a reunion of the divided people of God through a world-wide fellowship which will embrace "the children of Abraham—Jews, Christians and Moslems." In order to make this possible the church must recognize God's "unrevoked covenant with Israel, and Israel must recognize that in Christianity the God of Israel has revealed himself.

A Rabbi Looks at the Lord's Prayer

JAKOB J. PETUCHOWSKI

I

FROM TIME TO TIME I am playing a trick on the students who
are enrolled in my introductory course to Jewish Liturgy. I cannot do it every year because students tell such things to those
who succeed them; and I must, therefore, always wait until a
whole generation of students has left the campus. The trick is
played in connection with my discussion of the private prayers
of the ancient Rabbis, some of which were later incorporated
into the liturgy of Jewish public worship. In this connection,
we also discuss those prayers which, in an emergency, can take
the place of the statutory Prayer of the Eighteen Benedictions.

Here are some illustrations of the kinds of prayers about
which I am speaking:

Rabbi Eleazar would pray:

> May it be Your will, O Lord our God,
> to let dwell in our lot
> love and brotherhood,
> peace and friendship.
> May You make our borders rich in disciples.[1]

Rabbi Ḥiyya would pray:

> May it be Your Will, O Lord our God,
> that our Torah be our occupation,
> and that our heart may not be sick
> nor our eyes darkened.[2]

Rabbi Eleazar, as reported by Rabbi Pedath, would pray:

> May it be Your will, O Lord our God and God of our
>   ancestors,
> that no hatred against us enter the heart of anyone,
> and that no hatred of anyone enter our heart.
> May no jealousy of us enter the heart of anyone,
> and no jealousy of anyone enter our heart.
> May Your Torah be our occupation
> all the days of our life;
> and may our words be as supplications before You.[3]

For occasions when not enough concentration on the full
Eighteen Benedictions was possible, Rabbi Joshua suggested the
following prayer:

> Save, O Lord, Your people, the remnant of Israel.
> In every time of crisis, let their needs be before You.
> Praised are You, O Lord, who hearkens to prayer.[4]

Rabbi Eliezer suggested the following alternative prayer:

> Do Your will in heaven above,
> and grant equanimity to those who revere You here
>   below;
> and do that which is good in Your own eyes.
> Praised are You, O Lord, who hearkens to prayer.[5]

Others, again, favored this brief prayer:

> The needs of your people Israel are many,
> but their understanding is limited.
> May it be Your will, O Lord our God,
> to give to each one his sustenance,
> and to each body what it lacks.
> Praised are You, O Lord, who hearkens to prayer.[6]

It is in connection with the discussion of those and similar prayers that I will, on occasion, recite the following to my class:

> *abhinu shebashamayim,*
> *yithqaddash shemekha.*
> *tabho malkuthekha,*
> *ye'aseh retsonekha*
> *ka-asher bashamayim gam ba-arets,* etc.

After my recitation, I immediately ask my students: "Is that prayer part of the liturgy in the temples from which you come?" Some students start to grin at once, for they know enough Hebrew to understand that what I have been reciting in Hebrew translates as follows into English:

> Our Father in heaven,
> Thy name be hallowed;
> Thy kingdom come,
> Thy will be done,
> on earth as it is in heaven, etc.

But not all beginning students know enough Hebrew; and not all of them are sufficiently familiar with the liturgy of their hometown temples to know for sure what particular prayers are or are not recited there.

Thus it comes about that, every few years, there is a student in my class who, perhaps somewhat hesitatingly, raises his or her hand—only to be confronted by my fiendish comment: "So, you do come from a place of worship where the Lord's Prayer is part of the liturgy!" That is usually followed by general amusement—until I come to the aid of the hapless student by telling the class that their fellow student was more correct than they all realize. For, indeed, the various components of the Lord's Prayer do figure prominently in the Liturgy of the Synagogue, even though they may appear there in different parts of the service, and not, as they do in the major Christian prayer, joined to one another in one and the same prayer.

There is, however, one exception: There are many Jewish prayers which ask God to forgive our sins and the wrongs we have committed. But those prayers do not couple that request with the statement that *we* also forgive those who have wronged *us*. It is not that the sentiment would be foreign to a Jew. After all, in the Book of Ben Sira (or Ecclesiasticus), a Jewish work composed in the second pre-Christian century, and the only book of the Apocrypha which is occasionally quoted in the Talmud, we read:

> Forgive your neighbour his wrongdoing;
> then, when you pray, your sins will be forgiven.
>
> (Ecclus. 28:2)

And in a later Rabbinic work, the Midrash Tanhuma, we are told that if a person offends against his fellow and then says to him, "I have sinned," but the offended person does not forgive him, then it is the offended person, and not the original offender, who is called a "sinner."[7] The sentiment, then, is Jewish, all right, even though the Synagogue may lack a *liturgical* formulation of it.

Apart from that, however, there is not a phrase in the Lord's Prayer which cannot also be found in the prayers of the Synagogue. Those of my students, therefore, to whom the Hebrew version of the Lord's Prayer sounds somewhat familiar from their own hometown temples have—unwittingly, of course—beaten their fellow students to the quick recognition of the fact that the Lord's Prayer is a Jewish prayer, hewn from the same rock of Jewish devotion whence the prayers of the Synagogue are derived.

It may thus be possible that, as a rabbi and as a teacher of Jewish Liturgy, I might be able to help to shed some light on a number of aspects of the Lord's Prayer which might hitherto have been somewhat unclear even to our Christian friends.

Before we launch into an analysis of those aspects, however, we should, perhaps, define some terms which will be frequently invoked in our discussion.

II

By Lord's Prayer, I mean the prayer which, in Matthew 6:9–13 and in Luke 11:2–4, Jesus is said to have taught his disciples. I shall be using the New English Bible.

The version in Matthew reads as follows:

> Our Father in heaven,
> thy name be hallowed;
> thy kingdom come,
> thy will be done,
> on earth as in heaven.
> Give us today our daily bread (or our bread for the
>   morrow).
> Forgive us the wrong we have done,
> as we have forgiven those who have wronged us.
> And do not bring us to the test,
> but save us from the evil one (or from evil).
> (For thine is the kingdom and the power and the glory for
>   ever. Amen.)

That last verse is generally regarded in modern scholarship as a liturgical addition by the early Church, rather than as a component of the original Lord's Prayer.

The Luke version is much briefer and reads as follows:

> Father,
> thy name be hallowed;
> thy kingdom come.
> Give us each day our daily bread
> (or our bread for the morrow).
> And forgive us our sins,
> for we too forgive all who have done us wrong.
> And do not bring us to the test.

We shall here be mainly concerned with Matthew's version because, on account of its use in Christian worship, most people will have a greater familiarity with it. But we shall cast an occasional glance also at Luke's version.

Two other prayers should here be briefly identified. One of them is the *Qaddish* prayer, frequently spoken in the Synagogue. It begins as follows:

> Magnified and sanctified be His great name
> in the world which He has created according to His will.
> May He establish His kingdom
> during your life and during your days
> and during the life of the whole Household of Israel,
> speedily and at a near time,
> and say ye: Amen.
>> Amen. May His great name be praised
>> for ever and unto all eternity.[8]

The other prayer is the Prayer of the Eighteen Benedictions, which is *the* prayer *par excellence* of the Synagogue. Actually, for many a century now, it has been composed of *nineteen* benedictions, although the old name stuck. That is to say, on *weekdays* that prayer consists of nineteen benedictions. On the Sabbath and the festivals, it contains *seven* benedictions; and, for the Additional Service on the New Year festival, it actually contains *nine* benedictions. But we are here concerned with the weekday version, which the traditional Jew recites three times every day—just as the *Didache*, a Christian work of the early second century, tells the Christian to recite the Lord's Prayer three times a day.[9]

In the Eighteen Benedictions, the first benediction praises God, the Shield of Abraham. The second benediction praises God on account of His mighty acts. The third benediction celebrates God's holiness. When the Eighteen Benedictions are recited as part of public worship, that third benediction begins in the following manner:

We will sanctify Your name on earth,
even as they sanctify it in the highest heavens,
as it is written by the hand of Your prophet:
"And one called to another and said,
'Holy, holy, holy is the Lord of hosts,
the whole earth is full of His glory.'"

(Isa. 6:3)

Then come the petitionary prayers:

Benediction IV: The petition for knowledge and insight.
Benediction V: The petition for the ability to repent.
Benediction VI: The petition for divine forgiveness.
Benediction VII: The petition for redemption.
Benediction VIII: The petition for healing.
Benediction IX: The petition for agricultural abundance.
Benediction X: The petition for the ingathering of the exiles.
Benediction XI: The petition for righteous judges and God's rule.
Benediction XII: The petition for the disappearance of heretics.
Benediction XIII: The petition for God's mercy upon the righteous and upon the proselytes.
Benediction XIV: The petition for the rebuilding of Jerusalem.
Benediction XV: The petition for the Davidic messiah.[10]
Benediction XVI: The petition for the acceptance of prayer.
Benediction XVII: The petition for the acceptance of worship.
Benediction XVIII: Praise to the God to whom all thanks are due.
Benediction XIX: A prayer for peace.[11]

For people unable to memorize the whole Eighteen Benedictions—and the early Rabbis frowned on the writing down of prayers—[12] as well as for occasions when one could not fully concentrate on the complete text, there was also a shorter version, known as the "Essence of the Eighteen," which could be substituted for the Eighteen Benedictions. Different forms of the "Essence of the Eighteen" have been handed down by tradition. The most popular of them was taught by the Babylonian master, Mar Samuel, who need not necessarily have been its author, for he, living in the third century, could have mentioned a still earlier version. Samuel's arrangement calls for the regular text of the first three and the last three benedictions, while the intermediate twelve or thirteen benedictions are condensed into a single benediction. Thus, the "Essence of the Eighteen" actually consisted of *seven* benedictions—just as the Matthean version of the Lord's Prayer seems to consist of seven petitions. Samuel's text of the one intermediate benediction reads as follows:

> Give us understanding, O Lord our God,
>   that we may know Your ways.
> Circumcise our hearts that we may revere You.
> Forgive us, so that we may be redeemed.
> Keep us far from pain.
> Satiate us on the pastures of Your land,
> and gather our scattered ones from the four corners of
>   the earth.
> May those who go astray be judged according to Your
>   will,
> and wave Your hand over the wicked.
> May the righteous rejoice in the rebuilding of Your city,
> in the establishment of Your Temple,
> in the flourishing of the strength of Your servant David,
> and in the continuing dynasty of the son of Jesse, Your
>   anointed.
> Before we call, You answer us.
> Praised are You, O Lord, who hearkens to prayer.[13]

III

We are now ready to mention some of the problems concerning the provenance of the Lord's Prayer, with which scholars of Jewish and of Christian Liturgy have dealt. That there are *similarities* between the Lord's Prayer, on the one hand, and the *Qaddish* and the Eighteen Benedictions, particularly in their shortened version, on the other, is obvious. But all attempts to see in the Lord's Prayer an adaptation of the *Qaddish* and/or the Prayer of the Eighteen Benedictions are completely futile for one simple reason: However old some individual components of the Eighteen Benedictions may be—and some of them do indeed go back to the days of the Jerusalem Temple and even the second pre-Christian century—[14] the Prayer of the Eighteen Benedictions *as a liturgical unit* is *not* documented before the end of the first Christian century,[15] while the first reference to the *Qaddish* in Rabbinic literature is attributed to Rabbi Yosé in the middle of the second Christian century.[16] And, given the unfortunate relations between Church and Synagogue until very recent years, it is equally unlikely that the ancient Rabbis would have taken the Lord's Prayer as a model for their own liturgical creations. In any case, seeing that the Gospels themselves provide us with two different versions of the Lord's Prayer and that New Testament scholars are still arguing about the original language of the Lord's Prayer—Was it Hebrew, or was it Aramaic? A good case could be made for either!—we must also recognize the possibility that *both* versions, though they are *based* on the way in which Jesus taught his disciples to pray, may not represent the *ipsissima verba* of the teacher from Nazareth.

Any mutual dependence of the Christian prayer and the Jewish prayers would, therefore, be extremely hard, if not altogether impossible to prove—even though much ink has been used up in apologetic and polemic efforts to do just that. Certain phrases and certain *topoi,* some of them going back to the Hebrew Bible itself, were common in the religious world of ancient Palestine, where both the Lord's Prayer and the various prayers of the Rabbis originated. And the one as well as the others reflects the thoughts and the aspirations of pious Jews in that environment and at that time.

A somewhat more fruitful discussion would turn on the question of whether Jesus meant his prayer to be a private prayer, taking the place of a more formal liturgy—of, say, some prototype of the Eighteen Benedictions—or whether he meant his prayer to serve a liturgical function in Christian worship. Perhaps the best resolution of that problem would be to say that Jesus himself had intended his prayer to be an alternative to the pomp and circumstance of public worship, but that the rising Christian Church, already early in its development, used the Lord's Prayer liturgically and assigned it a role which would make it correspond to the Synagogue's Prayer of the Eighteen Benedictions.

The words of Matthew 6:5–6, preceding the Lord's Prayer in the New Testament, would make the first part of that solution plausible:

> Again, when you pray, do not pray like the hypocrites:
> they love to say their prayers standing up in synagogue
> and at the street-corners. . . .
> But when you pray, go into a room by yourself,
> shut the door, and pray to your Father who is there in
> the secret place; and your Father who sees what is secret
> will reward you.

Also, structurally, the Lord's Prayer bears a greater resemblance to the private prayers of the Rabbis than to the formal prayers of the Synagogue. It avoids the technical formulation of the *berakhah*, the synagogal form of the benediction: "Praised are You, O Lord, who . . ." At the same time, as the testimony of the second-century Didache indicates, and we have already referred to it, the Lord's Prayer was used liturgically quite early in the Church, and it was clearly meant to serve the function of a statutory daily prayer, just as the Prayer of the Eighteen Benedictions served that function in the Synagogue. That development is also indicated by the doxology that was placed at the end of the prayer: "For thine is the kingdom and the power and the glory, for ever. Amen."[17]

That, too, was a common development in the tradition of the Synagogue: Prayers, which were originally intended as private prayers and as devotional and optional supplements to the standard liturgy of public worship, came, in the course of time, to be incorporated as constituent parts of public worship itself. One can formulate it as a law of liturgical development: "One generation's devotional spontaneity becomes another generation's liturgical routine."[18] It is a law of liturgical development, so I am informed by reliable authorities on the history of Christian worship, which is as applicable to the development of the liturgy of the Church as it is to the development of the Jewish prayerbook.

Within the confines of a single essay, it is, of course, impossible to assemble illustrations which would show how every single phrase of the Lord's Prayer—with the single exception which we have noted before—beginning with the invocation of God as "Father," or "our Father in heaven," all the way to the plea that we be delivered from the evil one, or "from evil," as the older translations have it, is paralleled in the Liturgy of the Synagogue. Such gathering of illustrations is also not necessary within this particular context.[19] I would rather devote the remainder of the essay to the elucidation of some components of the Lord's Prayer, for which a knowledge of the world of Jewish prayer might be helpful.

IV

"Thy name be hallowed."

Names have meaning, occasionally even for us today. In ancient times, they were considered to be even more important, for name denoted essence, nature, character. When Moses asked to know God's name, he was told: *"Ehyeh asher ehyeh,* 'I am the One who is always present.' . . . 'This is My name for ever, and this is My title for all generations"* (Exod. 3:14–15). Another name by which God was known to Biblical Israel was "The Holy One of Israel."[20]

The Hebrew word for "holy" has the sense of being other, of being something out of the ordinary, of being totally different. Rudolf Otto has written perceptively of what "the Holy" means. On the one hand, it is the *mysterium tremendum.* It overpowers us and terrifies us. On the other hand, it is *fascinans.* It fascinates us, it attracts us, and it causes us to relate to it. Rudolf Otto has gathered his material about "the Holy" from all kinds of cultures and religions, and he noticed a strong similarity in the various perceptions of "the Holy." He also discovered that, on a very primitive level, "the Holy" has no necessary connection with the moral and ethical realm.[21]

The intimate connection between holiness and ethics, between the holy God and the moral demands made upon humanity, would seem to have been the great contribution which the Hebrew Prophets made to human civilization—as, for example, when Isaiah said:

> The Lord of hosts is exalted in judgment,
> and the holy God is sanctified in righteousness.
>
> (Isa. 5:16)

The hallowing, the sanctifying of God's name, of His essence, therefore, means that His moral qualities, as it were, are to be imitated by us humans in ever widening dimensions. Thus the Prophet Ezekiel, speaking in God's name, said:

> Thus will I magnify Myself, and I will sanctify Myself,
> and I will make Myself known in the eyes of many
>   nations;
> and they shall know that I am the Lord.
>
> (Ezek. 38:23)

That, of course, is the terminology we encounter at the very beginning of the *Qaddish* prayer ("Magnified and sanctified be His great name") and in the Lord's Prayer ("Thy name be hallowed"). And it follows quite logically that, in *both* prayers, the petition for the coming of God's Kingdom is placed immediately after. God's Kingdom will be established on earth, once God's holiness is perceived by all His human children, and once those human children will endeavor to live their lives in accordance with God's will.

V

"Thy kingdom come."

It will have been noted that, in Luke's version of the Lord's Prayer, Matthew's phrase "Thy will be done, on earth as in heaven" does *not* occur. Luke might here be closer to the original. My late teacher, the great Rabbi Leo Baeck, once explained in a lecture that the phrase "Thy will be done, on earth as in heaven" is not an additional *petition* at all, but merely a gloss on the phrase "Thy kingdom come." When a Jew hears the words "Thy kingdom come" he understands at once what the Kingdom of God is all about. It implies many things, to be sure. But, for a Jew, it goes without saying that the "Kingdom of God" means our doing God's will on earth. Yet when the Gospel was preached to the pagans of antiquity, they had no prior notion of what the words "Kingdom of God" mean, although they were, of course, familiar with all kinds of *other* human kingdoms. For their benefit, therefore, the words "Thy will be done, on earth as in heaven" were added as an *interpretation* of the phrase "Thy kingdom come."

Perhaps we need not even posit a pagan audience for whose benefit that explanatory gloss was added. For while it is true that, in most versions of the *Qaddish* prayer, no explanation of what is meant by "May He establish His kingdom" is added, there is one version of the *Qaddish*—recited both at a funeral and at the joyous occasion of completing the study of a whole tractate of the Talmud—that spells out in some detail what the eschatological expectations of Pharisaic-Rabbinic Judaism were in connection with the coming of God's Kingdom:

> Magnified and sanctified be His great name
> in the world which will be renewed,
> when He will resurrect the dead
> and raise them up to life eternal,
> when He will rebuild the city of Jerusalem,

and establish His Temple in her midst;
when He will uproot idolatry from the earth,
and restore the worship of the true God to its place.
Then the Holy One, praised by He, will reign
in His sovereignty and in His glory.
May that be during your life and during your days,
and during the life of the whole Household of Israel,
speedily and at a near time,
and say ye: Amen.[22]

Here, too, although at much greater length than in Matthew's version of the Lord's Prayer, we have a "spelling out" of what is meant by the coming of God's Kingdom. Yet we can hardly suppose that this "spelling out" was undertaken for the benefit of pagan listeners.

VI

The next petition in the Lord's Prayer is the petition for bread. Matthew has "Give us today our daily bread" *or* "our bread for the morrow." The exact translation of the Greek is a matter of serious and protracted scholarly debate. And Luke has "Give us each day our daily bread" *or* "our bread for the morrow."

It is not only that the exact meaning of the Greek words is in doubt here, for we do not find them elsewhere in this particular construction. But whatever those words *ton epiousion* might mean, there is an underlying *theological* problem that has bothered Christian thinkers from the days of the early Church Fathers to this day.

Let it be recalled that, later on in the sixth chapter of Matthew, in which the Lord's Prayer is found, Jesus criticizes those "of little faith" (Matt. 6:30) who are concerned with where tomorrow's bread may come from:

Look at the birds of the air; they do not sow and reap and store in barns, yet your heavenly Father feeds them.
You are worth more than the birds!

. . . .

So do not be anxious about to-morrow;
to-morrow will look after itself.
Each day has troubles enough of its own.

(Matt. 6:26, 34)

Interestingly enough, the very expression, "those of little faith," is applied by Rabbi Eliezer the Great to whose who worry about what they will eat the next day:

He who has bread in his basket, and says:
"What shall I eat to-morrow?,"
surely belongs to those who are of little faith.[21]

Now, if Jesus was so confident that God would look after his disciples, how are we to understand that he taught his disciples to ask God for their daily bread, or for the bread of the morrow? Moreover, if the Lord's Prayer is a messianic prayer, that is, a prayer suffused with the belief that the Kingdom of God was at hand, how could Jesus possibly have taught his disciples to pray for something as mundane as their daily bread?

Of such a kind were the questions which have bothered Christian interpreters of the Lord's Prayer since the early days of the Christian faith. Some of the Church Fathers interpreted the request for bread in a very ascetic sense. Thus Tertullian made the point that Jesus had commanded his disciples to ask *only* for bread, and not for wealth.[24] Hippolytus, commenting on Matthew 6:11, had this to say:

> For this reason we are enjoined to ask for what is sufficient for the preservation of the substance of the body: not luxury, but food which restores what the body loses, and prevents death by hunger; not tables to inflame and drive on to pleasures, nor such things as make the body wax wanton against the soul; but bread, and that, too, not for a great number of years, but what is sufficient for us today.[25]

Jean Carmignac, one of the great modern experts on the Lord's Prayer, devoted no less than 104 pages of his masterful volume, *Recherches sur le "Notre Père,"* to a discussion of what the word *artos* (Greek for "bread") and the words *ton epiousion* "really" mean within the context of the Lord's Prayer.[26] Is bread to be understood in a material sense? Or is it meant to be taken in a purely spiritual sense, in the way in which the Biblical manna, though obviously edible, was actually "bread from heaven" in a spiritual sense? Or is the expression polysemous—that is to say, could it signify *both* meanings? And what is the meaning of the "morrow"? Does it merely mean the day after today? Or does it refer to the Kingdom which is to come? Carmignac traces Christian interpretations of this clause of the Lord's Prayer from the early Church Fathers through modern Catholic and Protestant scholars. He himself holds to a polysemous interpretation. It is his conviction that the inner logic of the Lord's Prayer would be compromised, if Jesus had asked his disciples to pray *merely* for bread!

It would seem to me that this millennial Christian discussion about a simple prayer for our daily bread has always been due to the influence upon Christianity of Hellenistic ways of thinking, in which the spirit is exalted and the body is deprecated. That is why it was so hard for Christian exegetes to conceive of a Jesus who would teach his disciples to utter a request for their daily bread. At the very least, *via* the interpretation of manna as the "bread from heaven," Jesus must have alluded to the bread of the Eucharist!

But the need for such interpretations completely disappears when one sees the Lord's Prayer from the perspective of the whole world of Jewish prayer. It is true enough that the faithful Jew must not be overly concerned with what he will eat *tomorrow*, particularly if, as Rabbi Eliezer the Great has pointed out, one still has bread in one's basket. But that does not mean that one cannot, by means of such a petitionary prayer, express one's dependence on God for one's daily food!

In the Jewish Grace After Meals, the affirmation is made that, through God's great goodness, "we have never lacked food, and we never shall lack food."[27] But that does not prevent the Jew from praying in the same prayer:

Our God, our Father!
Feed us, nourish us, support us, sustain us![28]

Such a prayer, far from suggesting a lack of faith, actually reflects a mood of trust in God's providential care.

If, however, it be argued that, on account of its opening clauses, the Lord's Prayer is a *messianic* prayer and that Jesus would not have juxtaposed pre-messianic and messianic concerns, one would again point to the classical prayers of the Synagogue, in order to show that such a juxtaposition is not at all unusual in the realm of Jewish prayer. Take, for example, the ninth of the Eighteen Benedictions, as it was formulated in the early Palestinian Rite:

Bless, O Lord our God, this year for us,
and let it be good in all the varieties of its produce.
Hasten the year of the time of our redemption.
Grant dew and rain upon the face of the earth,
and satiate the world out of the treasuries of Your
    goodness.
And grant a blessing upon the work of our hands.
Praised are You, O Lord, who blesses the years.[29]

There is obviously a longing expressed in that prayer for a speedy messianic redemption. But just as obviously manifest in it is the awareness that we are dependent upon the earth's produce which God, through His blessings, bestows upon us. And there is no conflict between the two.

The same juxtaposition can be seen in another ancient Jewish prayer, the litany of *Abhinu Malkenu*, where we find the following combinations:

Our Father, our King! inscribe us in the book
    of redemption and salvation.
Our Father, our King! inscribe us in the book
    of maintenance and sustenance.[30]

And again:

> Our Father, our King! raise up the strength of Your
> Messiah.
> Our Father, our King! fill our hands with Your blessings.
> Our Father, our King! fill our storehouses with plenty.[31]

Admittedly, the tendency to spiritualize mundane requests can be found in Judaism, too. For example, the Patriarch Jacob's request at Beth-El for "food to eat and clothes to wear" (Gen. 28:20) is understood by one of the early Rabbis as a request for descendants who will serve as priests, and who, as such, will be entitled to eat the shewbread in the Temple and to wear priestly vestments.[32] The Rabbi who offered that interpretation must have been as embarrassed by the fugitive Patriarch's voicing of such mundane needs as those of food and clothing as many a Christian exegete has been by the petition for our daily bread in the Lord's Prayer.

But the story in the twenty-eighth chapter of the Book of Genesis makes sense without that Rabbinic interpretation; and the petition for our daily bread in the Lord's Prayer makes sense without the accumulated spiritualizing interpretations of the millennia. At any rate, it makes sense to a Jew in light of the millennial tradition of Jewish prayer—a tradition which contains among the various different versions of the *Qaddish* prayer also one, which, after praying for the coming of God's Kingdom, includes the request that

> upon Israel, and upon the Rabbis, and upon their disciples, and upon the disciples of their disciples, and upon all who engage in the study of the Torah in this or in any other place . . . may there be abundant peace, grace, lovingkindness, mercy, long life, ample sustenance and salvation from their Father who is in heaven.[33]

"Ample sustenance and salvation"! The juxtaposition of "salvation" and "ample sustenance" as gifts equally desired by the worshipper has never been considered problematical by the praying Jew. It is hard to see why it should have been a problem to the first Christians, who, after all, were Jews.

VII

We have by no means exhausted the Lord's Prayer. Nor have we exhausted the light which can be shed upon its meaning by the prayers of the Synagogue. Those prayers can, I believe, shed light also on such problems of New Testament exegesis as to whether the text should be translated "And do not bring us to the test" or as "And lead us not into temptation," and whether the text says: "But save us from the evil one" or "But deliver us from evil."

We *have*, however, exhausted the space for a single essay— although not, I would hope, without showing how a rabbi can look at the Lord's Prayer and find in it a spirit of prayer and an expression of devotion which are not at all foreign to him.

NOTES

1. B. *Berakhoth* 16b.
2. *Ibid.*
3. P. *Berakhoth* VI, 2, p. 7d.
4. *Mishnah Berakhoth* 4:4.
5. B. *Berakhoth* 29b.
6. *Ibid.*
7. *Midrash Tanhuma, Huqath* 46, ed. Buber, p. 63b.
8. Seligmann Baer, ed., *Seder 'Abhodath Yisrael* (Berlin, 1937), pp. 129f.
9. *Didache* 8:3.
10. The Palestinian Rite combined the petition for the rebuilding of Jerusalem with the petition for the Davidic Messiah, and thus had altogether *eighteen* benedictions. The Babylonian Rite, followed by all other rites, dealt with those two themes in two separate benedictions, thus having altogether *nineteen* benedictions. In our enumeration of the benedictions, we follow the arrangement of the Babylonian Rite.
11. Baer, *op. cit.*, pp. 87–104.
12. B. *Shabbath* 115b.
13. Baer, *op. cit.*, p. 108.
14. Cf. *Mishnah Tamid* 5:1; and see Ecclus. 51:12, i–xvi, in R. H. Charles, ed.,

The Apocrypha and Pseudepigrapha of the Old Testament (Oxford, 1913), Vol. I, pp. 514f.

15. B. *Berakhoth* 28b, 29a.

16. *Sifré, Ha-azinu*, #306, ed. Finkelstein, p. 342.

17. For the first part of the argument, see Joseph Heinemann, "The Background of Jesus' Prayer in the Jewish Liturgical Tradition," in *The Lord's Prayer and Jewish Liturgy*, ed. Jakob J. Petuchowski and Michael Brocke (New York, 1978), pp. 81–89. For the second part, see Gordon J. Bahr, "The Use of the Lord's Prayer in the Primitive Church," in Petuchowski and Brocke, *op. cit.*, pp. 149–55.

18. See Jakob J. Petuchowski, *Understanding Jewish Prayer* (New York, 1972), pp. 3–16.

19. See an example of a "Lord's Prayer" made up of Jewish parallels in Israel Abrahams, *Studies in Pharisaism and the Gospels*, 2nd ed. (New York, 1967), Pt. II, pp. 94–108, especially pp. 98f.

20. Isaiah 47.4 and often.

21. Rudolf Otto, *The Idea of the Holy* (New York, 1958).

22. Baer, *op. cit.*, p. 588.

23. B. *Sotah* 48b.

24. Alexander Roberts and James Donaldson, eds., *The Ante-Nicene Fathers* (Grand Rapids, MI, 1956), Vol. IV, p. 112.

25. Roberts and Donaldson, *op. cit.*, Vol. V, p. 194.

26. Jean Carmignac, *Recherches sur le "Notre Père"* (Paris, 1969), pp. 118–221.

27. Baer, *op. cit.*, pp. 554f.

28. Baer, *op. cit.*, p. 556.

29. Translated from the *Genizah* text as first published by Solomon Schechter in *JQR*, X (1898), reprinted in Jakob J. Petuchowski, ed., *Contributions to the Scientific Study of Jewish Liturgy* (New York, 1970), p. 476.

30. Baer, *op. cit.*, p. 110.

31. Baer, *op. cit.*, p. 111.

32. *Exodus Rabbah* XIX, 4.

33. Baer, *op. cit.*, p. 153.

The Catholic Church
and the Jewish People:
Evaluating the Results of
the Second Vatican Council

LAWRENCE E. FRIZZELL

The Second Vatican Council (1962–1965)

THE FOURTH AND LAST SESSION of the Second Vatican Council
ended in December, 1965. The Declaration on Non-Christian
Religions *(Nostra Aetate)* was promulgated by Pope Paul VI on
October 28, 1965, in the presence of a large crowd, including
four young Israelis. I had been showing these young people
around Rome and arranged for them to attend the ceremony in
Saint Peter's Basilica. The Pope's address was already recognized as an important moment in Catholic-Jewish relations,
but only in hindsight can we appreciate its full implication.

The Challenge of Change
Many will remember "good Pope John," proclaimed by the
pundits to be a "transition Pope" because of his venerable age.
Although his announcement on January 25, 1959, of an ecumenical council surprised everyone, few would have guessed its impact on the Church's life. Indeed, we still meet people who
reminisce about "the good old days" of the Church, blaming the
Council for what they consider to be the woes of our time. A review of the Church's history offers other examples of turmoil
after a council. Certainly many pastoral lessons can be learned
from the errors made in promoting those changes that affected

115

the life of the faithful. The change from Latin to the vernacular and the adaptation of the laws of fast and abstinence touch only the surface of spiritual reality, but such practices allowed for quick identification of a person's adherence to the Church. Did the clergy offer a careful explanation of the reasons for each change? Even when this was the case, much more attention should have been given to the time needed for an emotional response. Some of the clergy and a few religious women gave the impression that these changes meant that all was in flux. Certainly, the faithful in general deserve praise for their patience in this time of rapid transition. *Ecclesia semper reformanda!* The Church is always in need of reform! At any state of history, the Church is on a pilgrimage, in need of being purified of spot and wrinkle so that she might be holy and without blemish (Eph. 5:27). But how can change, however necessary, be appreciated as a sign of growth, not feared as a disruptive force? The Council Fathers of every age have been conscious of the challenge to reform without destroying. Like Jeremiah, they may see the need to pluck up or break down, but only as a prelude to the positive tasks of building and planting (Jer. 1:10). Thus, during the years of Vatican II, they and the preparatory Commissions used a prayer of Saint Isidore of Seville, composed in 619. It reads in part: "May You, who are infinite justice, never let us be disturbers of justice. Let not our ignorance induce us to evil, nor flattery sway us, nor material interest corrupt us. But unite our hearts to You alone . . . so that, with the gift of Your grace, we may be one in You and may in nothing depart from the truth."[1]

The Council began with this earnest plea, and its first published text was a "Message to Humanity." Just as Pope John XXIII's great encyclical *Pacem in Terris* (April 11, 1963) was addressed to "all people of good will," so already on October 20, 1962, all people and nations were greeted. The goal of the Council was stated simply: "In this assembly, under the guidance of the Holy Spirit, we wish to inquire how we ought to renew ourselves, so that we may be found increasingly faithful to the Gospel of Christ."[2]

For a considerable period of time before the Council was con-

vened, preparatory Commissions had worked to provide texts
for the discussion of the Council Fathers. Pope John XXIII, stim-
ulated by a visit of the Jewish historian Jules Isaac in 1960,
charged Augustin Cardinal Bea with the task of drafting a document on the Church's relation with the Jewish people. The
vagaries of the versions of this text have been traced by Msgr.
John M. Oesterreicher.[3] It finally emerged in 1965 as the key-
stone of the Council's Declaration on Non-Christian Religions.

Like all the sixteen texts promulgated by Pope Paul VI and
the Council Fathers, this Declaration is addressed to us Catholics, informing us about the Church's teaching and the demands
that flow from it for the faithful. The Church's description of
Jews, Moslems, Hindus, and others, however, does arouse their
interest, precisely because the Catholic Church is both numerous and worldwide. Because of the long and checkered history
of the Church's relationship with Jews and Judaism, they exhib-
ited considerable interest in this document during the Council
and afterwards. In the light of speculation about Jewish and
Arab influence at the Council, it is important to note that the
Church's concern was not merely to promote interfaith harmony. With regard to the Jewish people and their faith/culture,
the Church's words are in essence a search to express her own
integrity. Indeed, with regard to the Jewish people we modern-
day Catholics had a need "to renew ourselves, so that we may
be found increasingly faithful to the Gospel of Christ." This
need remains pertinent through subsequent decades, as work
springing from *Nostra Aetate* shows. No one has expressed this
better than Pope John Paul II, who said in his speech to the
Jewish community in Venezuela on January 15, 1985:

> I would like to confirm with the deepest conviction that the teaching
> of the church, given during the Second Vatican Council in the decla-
> ration of *Nostra aetate* . . . always remains for us, for the Catholic
> Church, for the episcopate . . . and for the pope, a teaching to which
> one must adhere, a teaching which one must accept not only as
> something relevant but even more, as an expression of the faith, as
> an inspiration of the Holy Spirit, as a word of divine wisdom.[4]

What did the Council Fathers emphasize concerning the

Church's relationship to the Jewish people? First, the Church sees a continuity from the time of Abraham and Sarah down to the immediate forebears of Jesus and the Apostles. Only with a deep knowledge of the Jewish Scriptures can Christians fully appreciate the content of Jesus' teaching and work. Of equal importance is the continuity of life and sustenance that is expressed in Saint Paul's image of the good olive tree.

Christian faith envisioned the work of Jesus, especially in his death-and-resurrection, as the source of reconciliation for human beings among themselves and with God the Father. In the drama of salvation, some leaders of the Jewish people opposed Jesus; however, in these activities, the Jewish people as such were not implicated. A large percentage of Jews lived outside the Holy Land at that time and, even among those in the Land, many did not encounter Jesus.

Jesus went to his death, not merely as one judged to be a criminal but as one who freely offered himself as the sacrificial victim for the forgiveness of the world's sins. Therefore, Christian teaching must focus on the mystery of Jesus' death as the sign of divine mercy.

The Church repudiates all persecution as contrary to the human rights of each individual, created in God's image. Anti-Jewish prejudice, known by the antiseptic term *anti-Semitism*, is rejected forcefully because of the Church's profound appreciation of all she has received from the Jewish people. The tragic past, with mutual misunderstanding and recriminations, should be put behind us. So the Council recommended dialogue based on biblical and theological study as the most solid foundation for true progress. Although there was no ulterior motive behind this recommendation for dialogue, the Church expresses the faith and hope derived from the Jewish Bible: a time when all peoples will praise God in unison, both in word and deed.[5]

Other Vatican II Texts on Catholic-Jewish Relations

The Declaration on Non-Christian Religions, and especially the section on the Jewish people, must be studied in the context of the other achievements of the Council.[6] Only then will we be able to evaluate its importance and understand how it came to be integrated into the daily spiritual life of Catholicism.[7] At the same time we will note the need for continued efforts to ensure that Catholics strive to overcome prejudice and search for justice and peace in their homes, communities, and workplaces. Of course, a number of important Christian statements were made to condemn anti-Semitism in the years between the Second World War and Vatican II, preceded in 1928 by a declaration of the Holy Office.[8] But even the 1948 and 1961 documents of the World Council of Churches did not bring about a great impact on those member Churches. Both Protestant and Jewish experts acknowledge that the implementation of Vatican II regarding Catholic-Jewish relations has provided others with a basis for emulation.[9] Although perfect harmony may be achieved only in Paradise, it is a commonplace perception that the climate *has* changed for the better; we now have the beginnings of an environment of trust within which problems can be aired and greater understanding achieved.

THE MAJOR CONSTITUTIONS

The centrality of the liturgy or public worship of the Church is affirmed in terms that draw from the biblical heritage. Christian life is described as a pilgrimage reminiscent of the Jewish tradition of focusing on Jerusalem and the Temple: "In the earthly liturgy we take part in a foretaste of that heavenly liturgy which is celebrated in the Holy City of Jerusalem to which we journey as pilgrims, where Christ is seated at the right hand of God" (*Liturgy #*8).[10] Throughout the course of history, "the liturgy is the summit toward which all the activity of the Church is directed; it is also the fount from which all her power flows" (#10).

Although the liturgical reforms that developed from the Second Vatican Council were intended to foster the spiritual life of Catholics, it is felicitous that the wider range of biblical readings provides many occasions for reflecting on our roots in the biblical and Jewish heritage. The Constitution on the Church *(Lumen Gentium)* develops biblical insights about the mystery of God's plan for salvation, beginning with the call of Abraham and coming to fulfillment in the work of Jesus (see Rom. 16:25–26). The image of the olive tree (from Rom. 11:13–26) in *Lumen Gentium* #6 and *Nostra Aetate* #4 helps Catholics to emphasize the continuity of God's plan. Then phrases like "new Covenant" and "new People of God" will not be interpreted as implying abrogation of the old Covenant or rejection of the Jewish people. These same terms, however, do teach the claim that a new reality has been achieved in the Paschal Mystery of Jesus' death-and-resurrection.

The Constitution on Divine Revelation situates the Sacred Scriptures within the liturgy, at the heart of the Church's life. The Council declared that the Jewish Scriptures (commonly known as the "Old Testament") are the true Word of God: "That is why these books, divinely inspired, remain permanently valuable" (#14). Lessons for every age can be discovered in all parts of these books, which deserve to be studied for themselves,[11] as well as in relation to the New Testament.

As in *Nostra Aetate* and elsewhere, the Constitution on the Church in the Modern World stresses the respect that is due to every human person: "Everyone should look upon his neighbor (without any exception) as another self, bearing in mind above all his life and the means necessary for living it in a dignified way." (#27). The challenge is laid on all Catholics to come to the aid of any person in need, especially the least fortunate. After providing principles that should inspire people to eliminate prejudice, the Council tried to foster greater human understanding: "Those also have a claim on our respect and charity who think and act differently from us in social, political and religious matters" (#28).

THE DECLARATION ON RELIGIOUS LIBERTY[12]

For Jews and other minorities in European and other countries with a Catholic majority, the touchstone for evaluating the Council's success is found in the Declaration on Religious Liberty. In the past the principle behind the exercise of authority in these nations had often been enunciated as follows: "Error has no right." The Council, "increasingly conscious of the dignity of the human person . . . searche[d] the sacred tradition and teaching of the Church, from which it drew forth new things that are always in harmony with the old" (#1). The result was the recognition that rights *reside in the human person* and people have inalienable rights, including the freedom of their conscience. Of course, every right has a concomitant responsibility, including the necessity of seeking the truth and embracing it (see #1).

The Council Fathers were well aware of the fact that Catholics in some lands were being persecuted for their faith and hoped that principles enunciated in this declaration (like the principles of the United Nations' 1948 Universal Declaration on Human Rights) would penetrate such regimes. By the same token, countries that follow the Church's guidance wholeheartedly would be required to provide freedom of assembly to religious minorities under their jurisdiction (#4).

The Council stated, "Parents have the right to decide in accordance with their own religious beliefs the form of religious upbringing which is to be given to their children" (#5). In the past a Jewish child, baptized because a Catholic thought the person to be in danger of death, could be taken from the parents' care.[13] Such a case would be extremely rare, but its poignancy caused great debates to arise. No longer will the parental right be scorned.

Religious freedom enables the Church to "enjoy in law and in fact those stable conditions which give her the independence necessary for fulfilling her divine mission" (#3). This mission was the subject of the Council's concern from the beginning, and it culminated in a Decree on the Church's Missionary Activity. Taking into account the principles enunciated in documents such as the Decrees on Ecumenism and Religious Liberty, the Council demanded that all Catholics and especially missionaries be educated to respect the rights of others and to present the Christian message in candor, truth, and charity. The burden of the past may weigh heavily upon the Church at times, but the search for authenticity in loving imitation of God demands this effort.

II. Post-Conciliar Developments

Introduction

There were no delusions among those who worked so hard to bring the Declaration on Non-Christian Religions to fruition. Augustin Cardinal Bea stated in a news release on October 20, 1965, that this Declaration was but "the beginning of a long and demanding way toward the arduous goal of a humanity whose members feel themselves truly to be sons of the same Father in heaven and act upon this conviction."[14]

Father Jean-Paul Lichtenberg, a French Dominican priest active in Jewish-Christian relations, commented that the Council document represents "a first stage of the difficult but necessary dialogue between the Church and Israel; a first invitation to Christians and Jews to understand each other better in order to love each other more sincerely, that is the true meaning of the present text. Another stage could be reached when the Church acknowledges Judaism as a living and effective religion. . . . Finally as a third stage the Church would have to recognize the State of Israel."[15] These "stages" will be discussed in the context of historical developments since 1965.

The term *dialogue* has been used on several levels by those who have sought reconciliation between Jews and Christians. In the years that preceded the Council, a number of Christian thinkers were attracted to Martin Buber's "I-Thou" understanding of authentic human encounter.[16] Without explicit reference to Buber, many consider that serious discussions between people of comparable background in their own faith traditions may be called "dialogue." Each person coming to the encounter is expected to respect the integrity of the other's commitment, so any intention of trying to convert the other person is set aside. Mutual understanding cannot be a condition of such dialogue, but should be one of its effects. The Council suggested that the focus of discussions might be the common spiritual heritage of Christians and Jews. Of course, scholars had shared over the decades, especially in the areas of biblical studies, Hebrew and Aramaic, archaeology, etc. This sharing was especially true of modern liberal Protestants and Jews in England and the United States. Soon after the Council, an increasing number of Catholic scholars entered creatively into these fields because the Council document on divine revelation reinforced the encouragement that Pope Pius XII had given to biblical scholars. Publications have included scholarly exchanges that, for the most part, show sensitivity to the work of others who come from different backgrounds. There is now a wealth of material, much of which is in English, upon which people from both communities can develop their understanding of the spiritual heritage that we share.[17]

After the Council the development of programs like "Living Room Dialogues" brought the good will fostered by the Council to the local parish and synagogue communities, especially in the cities and suburbs of the United States. At times these groups would include both Catholics and Protestants; for the most part, the Jewish traditions represented were Reform and Conservative. Both on the scholarly and grassroots levels, Orthodox Jews for the most part adhered to a statement by Rabbi Joseph B. Soloveitchik, the highly respected teacher at Yeshiva University in New York. He proposed discussions on humanitarian and cultural endeavors and man's moral values, but not on theology as such.[18]

The education of clergy and laity for a deeper understanding of the Council's synthesis of Catholic theology began almost immediately. At times there was resistance, perhaps only a half-hearted response to certain changes in the liturgy, ecumenical attitudes, etc. Teachers in seminaries and other houses of spiritual and theological formation often took more extensive training than the parish clergy.[19] Gradually new programs for the education of children were developed. Usually these were monitored carefully with regard to the portrayal of Jews, Protestants, and others.[20]

Implementing Nostra Aetate *by the Vatican*

In early 1966 Father Cornelius Rijk, a scholar from Holland, was appointed to work for Catholic-Jewish relations within the Secretariat for Christian Unity. In April, 1969, he convened a meeting of twenty-one Catholics from fourteen countries for the purpose of preparing a "schema" or text that would be background for the plenary session of Bishops belonging to the Secretariat. The text that emerged from the Bishops' meeting in November, 1969, was published later,[21] but there was a frustrating delay, during which time Father Rijk resigned. In October, 1974, Pope Paul VI set up a Commission for Religious Relations with the Jews and on December 1, 1974, "Guidelines and Suggestions for Implementing the Conciliar Declaration *Nostra Aetate*" was promulgated by Cardinal Willebrands.[22]

Already the National Conference for Catholic Bishops and several dioceses in the United States and Europe had offered Guidelines for the faithful, taking into account national and local needs.[23] The work of the Council was further enhanced by the Vatican Guidelines, especially in parts of the world where little initiative had been taken. After a preamble, there are four sections in "Guidelines": dialogue, liturgy, teaching, and joint social action.

What is new? The milestone in Catholic-Jewish relations expressed in the Conciliar Declaration is set in the historical context of the *Shoah*, often designated as "the Holocaust." All forms of anti-Semitism and discrimination are condemned: "Christians must strive to acquire a better knowledge of the basic components of the religious tradition of Judaism; they must strive to learn by what essential traits the Jews define themselves in the light of their own religious experience."[24] Certainly the Church here recognizes Judaism to be a living religion, as Father Lichtenberg desired. The text explains: "Dialogue demands respect for the other as he (or she) is, above all respect for his (or her) faith and religious conviction."[25] Here principles articulated by the Council with regard to Christian ecumenism are applied to Catholic-Jewish relations. The same is true regarding the mission of the Church to present Christ to the world: "Lest the witness of Catholics to Jesus Christ should give offense to Jews, they must take care to live and spread their Christian faith while maintaining the strictest respect for religious liberty."[26] Points from the Constitutions on the Sacred Liturgy and Divine Revelation are the basis for insisting that the clergy be alert to the Jewish heritage and take great care not to reiterate stereotypes or generalizations about Jews.

The acceptance of Judaism as a living religion is reinforced: "The history of Judaism did not end with the destruction of Jerusalem, but rather went on to develop a religious tradition . . . rich in religious values."[27] Specialized research is encouraged: "wherever possible, chairs of Jewish studies will be created, and collaboration with Jewish scholars encouraged."[28] Improved Jewish and Christian relations should have results that go far beyond the two communities as such: "Love of the same God must show itself in effective action for the good of humankind."[29]

On June 24, 1985, the same Vatican Commission promulgated "Notes on the Correct Way to Present the Jews and Judaism in Preaching and Catechesis."[30] The task of transmitting the faith on every level, both in liturgy and in the classroom, must be approached with learning and care. More than twice as long as the 1974 "Guidelines" (thirteen printed pages compared with six), "Notes" has six sections: religious teaching and Judaism, relations between the Old and New Testaments, Jewish roots of Christianity, the Jews in the New Testament, the liturgy, and Judaism and Christianity in history.

Quoting Pope John Paul II's speech to Catholic experts on the Church's relation with the Jews (March 6, 1982), "Notes" stresses the unique relation between Christianity and Judaism; thus the Jewish people and Judaism should occupy an essential place in Christian education ("their presence there is essential and should be organically integrated").[31] Pope John Paul II has spoken more profoundly and more often about the Church's relationship to the Jewish people and Judaism than any of his predecessors.[32] Although Catholics do not expect Jewish theologians to agree, it is extremely important that we recognize that the two religions are "linked together at the very level of their identity." Their bond is "founded on the design of the God of the Covenant." As Bishop Mejia, then Secretary of the Commission, explained: "It is a practical impossibility to present Christianity while abstracting from the Jews and Judaism, unless one were to suppress the Old Testament, forget about the Jewishness of Jesus and the Apostles, and dismiss the vital cultural and religious context of the primitive Church."[33] Unfortunately, he did not comment on the awkward clause: "It should be organically integrated." I would suggest that only a thorough portrayal of the main themes of Jewish thought and practice, through the prism of the Sadducee, Pharisee, and Essene movements, can achieve this ideal of "integration." It is not enough merely to describe the context necessary to understand given passages in the New Testament, although this is a beginning. An understanding of the dynamic vitality of Jewish life and thought will have the effect of removing the basis for stereotypes of Judaism as moribund and Jews as legalistic and hypocritical. An added benefit will be the elucidation of the places where the teaching of Jesus builds on the common insights of his contemporaries into the biblical heritage and where Jesus and the Church made unique contributions.

Another passage of the Pope's speech of March 6, 1982, is quoted: "To assess the common patrimony carefully in itself and with due awareness of the faith and religious life of the Jewish people *as they are professed and practiced still today,* can greatly help us to understand better certain aspects of the life of the Church."[34] "Notes" draws this conclusion: "It is a question then of *pastoral* concern for a still living reality closely related to the Church." The Holy Father implied that all Catholics should have this positive appreciation of Judaism. In Mainz on November 17, 1980, he had made this point already in a ponderous German sentence: "The first dimension of this dialogue, that is the meeting between the people of God of the Old Covenant, never revoked by God (see Rom. 11:29), and that of the New Covenant, is at the same time a dialogue within our Church . . . between the first and second part of her Bible." The Old Covenant has never been revoked by God! The implications of this statement for Catholics are considerable and have been discussed at length.[35] "Notes" discusses the relationship between the two Testaments in detail, differing from a theory of Franz Rosenzweig (1889–1929) that God has two Covenanted communities that complement each other: "The Church and Judaism cannot then be seen as two parallel ways of salvation and the Church must witness to Christ as the Redeemer for all, while maintaining the strictest respect for religious liberty."[36]

In the final section, "Notes" reiterates the truth that Judaism is a living faith: "The history of Israel did not end in 70 A.D. It continued, especially in the numerous Diaspora which allowed Israel to carry to the whole world a witness—often heroic—of its fidelity to the one God. . . . While preserving the memory of the land of their forefathers at the heart of their hope (Passover Seder)."[37] Then "Notes" offers a comment related to Father Lichtenberg's third stage: "The existence of the State of Israel and its political options should be envisaged not in a perspective which is in itself religious, but in their reference to the common principle of international law."[38] The Vatican Commission for Religious Relations with the Jews does not consider political questions, since these belong to the Secretary of State. The Pope has spoken on a number of occasions about the necessity for the State of Israel to have secure borders and peace with her neighbors; at the same time he mentions the legitimate human rights of Palestinian Arabs and of the need to take their aspirations into account. Any solution to a question of debate between people of two religious traditions can be resolved only by adherence to the principles of international law. Recent years have been a time of grave danger to Israel and its people. We pray fervently that current initiatives will achieve what has so long eluded the peoples of the Near East: a just and lasting peace that will permit Jews and Arabs to grow into a dialogue toward mutual understanding.

Why does the Vatican not recognize the state of Israel? This question comes again and again from Jews, whether they are interested in dialogue or not. In a way, this questioning may be interpreted as an indication of a Jewish perception of the Pope's authority. If only he would act, the world would acknowledge Israel, especially the Arab countries. Would that this were true!

The first point that must be stressed is that the Vatican *does* recognize the state of Israel. Although Pope Paul VI paid only a brief visit to the shores of Lake Gennesareth in 1964, the prime minister and other high officials of Israel's government have been received at the Vatican on several occasions. There is, however, yet to be the *full* diplomatic relations that includes the exchange of ambassadors.

The reasons given by representatives of the Secretary of State for the lack of full diplomatic relations are as follows: (1) The Vatican normally enters full diplomatic relations only with nations whose boundaries are clearly defined; thus there is no ambassador sent to Jordan or Israel; (2) There is grave concern for the situation of the small Christian minorities in Moslem lands, especially in Syria, Egypt, and Iraq; (3) There is a concern for the status of Jerusalem and the holy places, with access for all. I would add another: The Pope is not only concerned about peace but also about ways in which he can use the good offices of Vatican diplomacy to foster peace. Would Israeli leaders be interested in an ongoing and developing relationship with the Vatican in which frank discussions of goals and policies would be part of the agenda? The Vatican ambassador would not have a deciding influence in any issues, but perhaps his voice would be worth listening to from time to time.

My personal hope is that the present peace initiatives will bring a solution to all the long-standing questions about the borders of Israel with Jordan and Syria, the status of a united Jerusalem as the capital of Israel, and a way in which Palestinians can achieve human and civil rights. Then, within a short time we could hope for an exchange of ambassadors between the Vatican and Israel. Although the third stage in Catholic-Jewish relations will not lead immediately to world peace, every positive step is laden with enormous significance.

The Church is not identified with the Vatican; the relationship between Catholics and the 106-acre Vatican State is not analogous to that of Diaspora Jews to Israel. The leadership of the Church does not count merely on diplomatic endeavors to cope with the world's problems, or with the problems of Catholics. Rather, the Church's desire, continuing the work of the Council, is to deepen the relationship of the faithful with God. Then from that grace-filled understanding of herself, the Church hopes to move with humility and courage to face the challenges of the age.

Recent Developments

There have been some misunderstandings and tensions between the Jewish and Catholic communities over the decades. Predictably, these points of friction have been considered much more newsworthy by the mass media than the careful work that has been developing across many countries. Neither the "incidents" nor the positive steps can be traced at length here.[39]

From September 3 to September 6, 1990, the thirteenth meeting of the Vatican Commission for Religious Relations with the Jews and the International Jewish Committee on Interreligious Consultation took place in Prague, Czechoslovakia.[40] The papers and discussions focused on anti-Semitism in Christian history, the Shoah, and contemporary developments in Eastern Europe. There was a joint statement at the end of the conference offering the following highlights: "The Catholic delegates condemned anti-Semitism as well as all forms of racism as a sin against God and humanity, and affirmed that one cannot be authentically Christian and engage in anti-Semitism" and the fact "that anti-Semitism has found a place in Christian thought and practice calls for an act of *teshuvah* (repentance) and of reconciliation on our part."[41]

New political developments in Eastern and Central Europe allow the Church a freedom that it has not possessed since the

1930s. The teaching of the Second Vatican Council and later documents can now be translated and published for wide dissemination. The Prague statement offers a number of suggestions to guide the Bishops and other authorities in their educational efforts.

Two more recent events are also significant: the celebration of the twenty-fifth anniversary of *Nostra Aetate* (in Rome on December 5, 1990) and the Pastoral Letter of the Polish Bishops on Jewish-Catholic Relations (dated November 30, 1990, and read in all Polish Churches on January 20, 1991).[42] Members of the same groups who met in Prague in September came to Rome for a one-day ceremonial confirmation of the Prague statement. Pope John Paul's speech made several important points that deserve our attention. The foundation for this celebration was "nothing other than the divine mercy which is guiding Christians and Jews to mutual awareness, respect, cooperation and solidarity."[43] This wording reminds us of the prayer by Saint Isidore of Seville, which was recited at the beginning of every session of the Second Vatican Council. The work of building upon the declaration *Nostra Aetate* is not merely an exercise in Christian-Jewish relations, laudable as that is. It is an act of service—to God and to divine truth.

The Pope suggested that the strength of the Declaration came from its approach "to all peoples from a *religious* perspective." This perspective is "the deepest and most mysterious of the many dimensions of the human person." Perhaps he had in mind the 1991 World Day of Peace Message, issued in December, 1990, in anticipation of the new year. The message is entitled "Respect for Conscience: Foundation for Peace."[44]

This openness of *Nostra Aetate* is "anchored in a high sense of the absolute singularity of God's choice of a particular people, His own people, Israel according to the flesh, already called 'God's Church'" (citing Vatican II, *Lumen Gentium* #9). The biblical passages cited indicate that the seemingly incongruous term "Church" refers to the *qahal*, the convocation by God's Word of the people gathered at the foot of Mount Sinai. Then the Pope stressed that the Church's self-definition must include an insight into her relation with the descendants of Abraham by stating, "The Church is fully aware that Sacred Scripture bears witness that the Jewish people, this community of faith and custodian of a tradition thousands of years old, is an intimate part of the 'mystery' of revelation and salvation." Probably he was alluding to the clause in John 4:22 "for salvation is from the Jews."[45] The *mysterion*, the divine plan that was unfolded slowly to guide human beings to their true goal in history, is not abstract but rather clothed in the body of Israel.

The Pope then pointed to the place of the Scriptures *(Miqra)* and especially Torah in the Jewish tradition. "You live in a special relationship with the Torah, the living teaching of the living God," said the Pope. "You study it with love in Talmud Torah, so as to put it into practice with joy." The Constitution on Divine Revelation of the Second Vatican Council already stresses that "the true word of God is found in the Old Testament: these books, written under divine inspiration, remain permanently valuable" (#14). The Pope's words showed his grasp of what the Torah and the two other parts of the Hebrew Bible mean to the Jews—and certainly this paragraph should be used by all Catholic teachers.

What characterizes Jews from the religious point of view? The Pope responded: "God, his holy Torah, the synagogal liturgy and family traditions, the Land of Holiness, at whose center lies Jerusalem." Dialogue must not overlook the Shoah. Pope John Paul II endorsed the Prague statement vigorously and asked for vigilance to protect "human and religious rights." The Pastoral Letter of the Polish Bishops is expressly a continuation of the Church's effort to interpret and apply the contents of *Nostra Aetate* to life in Poland. It is rooted in documents of the Universal Church and provides a fine summary of *Nostra Aetate* and quotes teachings of Pope John Paul II frequently. The idea that Christians replaced or superseded the Jewish people is rejected, as is the deicide charge. The history of Polish-Jewish relations is sketched briefly, with considerable detail given to the Shoah. As the "Avenue of Righteous Gentiles" in Jerusalem proclaims, many Poles attempted to save Jews. No mention is made in this letter that each person realized that, if caught, he or she *and his or her entire family* would be killed by the Nazis. Only in Poland was the penalty so severe.

Indifference on the part of some was noted by the Bishops: "We are especially disheartened by those among Catholics who in some way were the cause of the death of Jews. They will forever gnaw at our conscience on the social plane . . . we must also ask forgiveness of our Jewish brothers and sisters."[46] Picking up a thought from *Nostra Aetate,* the Bishops deplored "all the incidents of anti-Semitism which were committed at any time and by anyone on Polish soil." They went on to say, "We do this with the deep conviction that all incidents of anti-Semitism are contrary to the spirit of the Gospel and . . . remain opposed to the Christian vision of human dignity."

These efforts to instruct Catholics will accomplish a great deal if the spirit and content of this pastoral letter become integrated into the Church's preaching of the Gospel to adults and the Church's instruction of children. The recent visit of Polish president Lech Walesa to Israel showed that the Church's teaching has resonances in public life and international affairs.[47]

Conclusion

This sketch of the Council's teaching in relation to the Jewish people and their place in the Church's self-definition has shown how profoundly the biblical vision influences the life of Catholics. The process of renewal is the result of many influences, but the most profound of these is the impact of God's Word on the Church and her members. The subsequent official documents that have been included in this review are but representative of the intense and extensive work accomplished by people of good will in many nations. The spirit of the Council is certainly being felt throughout the world; in Catholic-Jewish relations this is true especially in places with a large Jewish population or a long Jewish history. This is, however, not merely a matter of intercultural harmony or interfaith relations; rather the new attitude of appreciation for Judaism and the Jewish people involves a rediscovery of the Church's roots.[48] Certainly, unceasing efforts to overcome anti-Jewish prejudice continue to be extremely important; yet this work is deepened by being placed within the context of the Church's search to express her own faith and practice. Anti-Semitism was an aspect of Jewish-Gentile relations long before Christianity emerged. The elimination of all such prejudice will require ongoing vigilance, so the Catholic community must take to heart the realization that anti-Semitism is a sin against God and humanity.[49] Would that the phrase "Christian anti-Semitism" be recognized by all to be an oxymoron!

One can but wish that the sentiments of the following words of Pope John Paul II would become universally true:

> The relationship between Jews and Christians has been radically improved in these years. Where there was ignorance and therefore prejudice and stereotype, there is now a growing mutual knowledge, appreciation and respect. There is, above all, love between us: that kind of love I mean, which is for both of us a fundamental injunction of our religious traditions and which the New Testament has received from the Old.[50]

NOTES

1. Walter Abbott, ed., *The Documents of Vatican II* (New York: Corpus Books, 1966) xxii.

2. *Ibid.*, 3–4.

3. See his study in Herbert Vorgrimler, ed., *Commentary on the Documents of Vatican II* (New York: Herder and Herder, 1969), vol. 3, pp. 1–136; J. M. Oesterreicher, *The New Encounter Between Christians and Jews* (New York: Philosophical Library, 1986) 103–295.

4. This text is cited in the "Pastoral on Jewish-Catholic Relations," of the Polish Bishops; the latter is published in *Origins* 20 (February 14, 1991): 593.

5. This summary might be supplemented by commentaries on *Nostra Aetate* #4.

6. Addressing delegation of the American Jewish Committee on March 16, 1990, Pope John Paul made this very point: "Although the Catholic teaching concerning Jews and Judaism is summarized in *(Nostra Aetate)* #4, many of its fundamental elements are also present in other documents of the Council. . . . Perhaps

the time has come, after 25 years, to make a systematic study of the Council's teaching on this matter" (*Osservatore Romano*, Italian ed. March 17, 1990).

7. For a detailed analysis of the Council documents, see my essay entitled "The Teaching of the Second Vatican Council on Jews and Judaism," to be published as part of a volume edited by James H. Charlesworth.

8. See Helga Croner, ed., *Stepping Stones to Further Jewish-Christian Relations* (New York: Stimulus Books, 1977).

9. Less has been accomplished in Orthodox Christian circles; see George Papademetriou, *Essays on Orthodox Christian-Jewish Relations* (Bristol, Ind.: Wyndham Press, 1990).

10. See A. Finkel, "Jerusalem in Biblical and Theological Tradition—a Jewish Perspective," in *Evangelicals and Jews in an Age of Pluralism*, ed. Marc Tanenbaum, et al. (Grand Rapids: Baker House, 1984) 140–62, and my article, "Pilgrimage: A Study of the Biblical Experience," *Jeevadhara* 71 (1982): 358–67.

11. For the themes of Torah and ecology, see my articles, "Law at the Service of Humankind," *SIDIC* 19 (#3-1986): 4–7, and "Humanity and Nature According to the Jewish Scriptures," *SIDIC* 22 (#3-1988): 5–8.

12. See Pietro Pavan's commentary in Herbert Vorgrimler, ed., *Commentary on the Documents of Vatican II* (New York: Herder and Herder, 1969) vol. 4, pp. 49–86; Walter Burghardt, ed., *Religious Freedom: 1965 and 1975* (New York: Paulist, 1977). Reflections on this Declaration have been drawn from my essay, "Teachings of the Second Vatican Council." See also Robert Gordis, "Religious Liberty: A Jewish Perspective," in *Fifteen Years of Catholic-Jewish Dialogue, 1970–1985* (Rome: Libreria Editrice Vaticana, 1988), 157–79.

13. See Giorgio Romano, "Mortara Case," in *Encyclopedia Judaica* 12 (1967): 354–55, and Bertram W. Korn, *The American Reaction to the Mortara Case* (Cincinnati: Jewish Archives, 1957). Another such problem occurred in World War II. Parents who died in a Nazi concentration camp had entrusted two infant sons to a Catholic; she had them baptized. See Edward Flannery, "The Finaly Case," in *The Bridge*, ed. J. M. Oesterreicher, 1 (1955): 292–313.

14. Oesterreicher, art. cit. 130.

15. *Ibid.*, The original article appeared in *Esprit* (June, 1966); the quotation is from p. 1178.

16. See John M. Oesterreicher, *The Unfinished Dialogue: Martin Buber and the Christian Way* (New York: Philosophical Library, 1986); Harold Stahmer, "*Speak That I May See Thee!*" *The Religious Significance of Language* (New York: Macmillan, 1968).

17. See Lawrence Boadt et al., eds., *Biblical Studies: Meeting Ground of Jews and Christians* (New York: Paulist, 1980); Clemens Thoma and Michael Wyschogrod, eds., *Understanding Scripture: Explorations of Jewish and Christian Traditions of Interpretation* (Mahwah, N.J.: Paulist, 1987); and Val Ambrose McInnis, ed., *Renewing the Judaeo-Christian Wellsprings* (New York: Crossroad, 1987).

18. Soloveitchik's article is reprinted in Norman Lamm and Walter Wurzburger, eds., *A Treasury of Tradition* (New York: Hebrew Publishing, 1967) 55–80; see esp. pp. 78–80.

19. Eugene J. Fisher, *Seminary Education and Christian-Jewish Relations* (Washington, D.C., 1988); Walter Burghardt, "Of Their Race is the Christ: How to Preach About the Jews," in *Preaching: The Art and the Craft* (Mahwah, NJ: Paulist, 1987) 139–58; Bishops' Committee on the Liturgy, *God's Mercy Endures Forever: Guide-*

lines on the Presentation of Jews and Judaism in Catholic Preaching (Washington, DC: United States Catholic Conference, 1989).

20. See John Pawlikowski, *Catechetics and Prejudice* (New York: Paulist, 1973); Eugene J. Fisher, *Faith Without Prejudice* (New York: Paulist, 1977); and Rose Thering, *Jews, Judaism, and Catholic Education* (South Orange, NJ: Seton Hall University, 1986).

21. Croner, *Stepping Stones*, 2–11.

22. *Ibid.*, 11–16.

23. *Ibid.*, 16–68.

24. *Ibid.*, 11.

25. *Ibid.*, 12.

26. *Ibid.*, 12.

27. *Ibid.*, 14.

28. *Ibid.*, 15. The Chair of Judeo-Christian Studies at Tulane University in New Orleans was established in 1969. The pioneer work of Msgr. John M. Oesterreicher in Vienna and at Seton Hall University, South Orange, N.J., was the basis for the Master's program in Judeo-Christian Studies that was initiated at Seton Hall in 1975.

29. *Ibid.*, 15.

30. The text is found in Helga Croner, ed., *More Stepping Stones to Jewish-Christian Relations* (Mahwah, N.J.: Paulist, 1985) 220–32 and in Eugene J. Fisher and Leon Klenicki, eds., *In Our Time: The Flowering of Jewish-Catholic Dialogue* (Mahwah, N.J.: Paulist, 1990) 38–50.

31. Fisher and Klenicki, *In Our Time*, 39.

32. Papal statements and work of the Commission for Religious Relations with the Jews are presented in the *Information Service* of The Pontifical Council for Promoting Christian Unity; many are found in *Origins* (Washington, DC: Catholic News Service).

33. This text is found in Fisher and Klenicki, *In Our Time*, 54.

34. *Ibid.*, 49.

35. See Norbert Lohfink, *The Covenant Never Revoked: Biblical Reflections on Christian-Jewish Dialogue* (Mahwah, N.J.: Paulist, 1991).

36. Fisher and Klenicki, *In Our Time*, 41. See Eugene J. Fisher, "Covenant Theology and Jewish-Christian Dialogue," *American Journal of Theology and Philosophy* 9 (1988): 5–39 and articles in *SIDIC* (Rome) 23 (#3-1990).

37. *Ibid.*, pp. 48–49.

38. *Ibid.*, 49. See Eugene J. Fisher, "The Holy See and the State of Israel: The Evolution of Attitudes and Policies," *Journal of Ecumenical Studies* 24 (1987): 191–211; George Irani, *The Papacy and the Middle East: The Role of the Holy See in the Arab-Israeli Conflict, 1962–1984* (Notre Dame, Ind.: University of Notre Dame Press, 1986).

39. See Eugene J. Fisher, A. James Rudin, and Marc H. Tanenbaum, eds., *Twenty Years of Jewish-Catholic Relations* (Mahwah, N.J.: Paulist, 1986); Eugene J. Fisher, "Mysterium Tremendum: Catholic Grapplings with the Holocaust and Its Theological Implications," *SIDIC* 22 (#1-2, 1989): 10–15. The discussion of anti-Semitism in "The Church and Racism: Toward a More Fraternal Society," issued by the Pontifical Council on Justice and Peace (November 3, 1988) is especially noteworthy.

40. The proceedings of earlier meetings have been edited by The International

Catholic-Jewish Liaison Committee under the title *Fifteen Years of Dialogue, 1970–1985* (Rome: Libreria Editrice Vaticana, 1988).

41. The text is published in the *Information Service* of the Pontifical Council for Promoting Christian Unity 75 (1990): 173–178; *Catholic International* 2 (February 15–28, 1991): 159–164.

42. Both events are linked with the Prague meeting, although the letter of the Polish bishops builds on work of several years. See note 4.

43. See *Catholic International* 2 (February 15–28, 1991): 167.

44. The text is published in *Origins,* 472–476.

45. See Otto Betz, "'To Worship God in Spirit and in Truth': Reflections on John 4:20–26," in *Standing Before God: Studies in Honor of John M. Oesterreicher* (New York: Ktav, 1981) 53–72.

46. On April 28, 1980, the Catholic Bishops of Germany stated: "In Germany we have particular cause to ask forgiveness of God and of our Jewish brethren. Even though we thankfully remember that many Christians supported the Jews, often at great sacrifice, we may not, nor do we wish to, either forget or suppress what has been done by our nation to the Jews. We call to mind what the Bishops' Conference at Fulda in 1945, their first meeting after the war, proclaimed: 'Many Germans, including Catholics, allowed themselves to be deluded by the false teaching of National Socialism, and remained indifferent to the crimes against human freedom and human dignity; many abetted the crimes, through their behavior, many became criminals themselves. A heavy responsibility rests on those, who by reason of their position, knew what was happening in our country, who through their influence could have prevented such crimes and did not do so, and so made these crimes possible, and by so doing, declared their solidarity with criminals.'" The citation is from Rabbi Jack Bemporad's presentation in Rome on December 6, 1990, published in *Catholic International* 2 (February 15–28, 1991): 170.

47. The first visit of a Polish leader to Israel was reported by *The New York Times*, May 21, 1991, p. A5.

48. See John M. Oesterreicher, *The Rediscovery of Judaism: A Re-examination of the Conciliar Statement on the Jews* (South Orange, N.J.: Seton Hall University, 1971).

49. The Prague statement (*Catholic International* 2 [February 15–28, 1991]: 162).

50. Audience with Jewish leaders on February 15, 1985, cited in the Prague statement (*ibid.,* 163).

Heidegger's Philosophy
of Religion

JOHN MACQUARRIE

I HAVE CHOSEN as the theme of this essay "Heidegger's Philosophy of Religion." It is just four years since Martin Heidegger died at the age of eighty-seven, and, of course, for many, many years he had held the Chair of Philosophy in the University of Freiburg. And probably no modern philosopher has exerted such an influence on the theology of the twentieth century as has Martin Heidegger. Bultmann, Tillich, Rahner, are among the many outstanding theologians who are all deeply in his debt. It is not difficult to discover what theologians have owed to Heidegger. But what is much more difficult, and what I intend to explore in this essay, is to discover just what Heidegger himself thought of theology and religion in general.

It is well known that in his youth Heidegger spent some time in a Jesuit seminary. And many years later, when he was an established, world-famous philosopher, he declared, "Without my theological origin, I would never have attained to the way of philosophical thinking."[1] During most of his career, however, he kept theology at a distance. He believed that the tasks of the theologian and of the philosopher are quite different. He did not encourage much in the way of dialogue. We find him saying, "Someone who has experienced theology in his own roots, both the theology of the Christian faith and philosophical theology, would today rather remain silent about God when he is speaking in the realm of philosophy."[2]

Heidegger's own aloofness from theological questions has led to some questioning of the legitimacy of employing his philoso-

137

phy in theological work. But one might say his own attitude toward theology is irrelevant to the application of his ideas. He himself believed that language always says more than the person who speaks it means to express, and that sometimes the interpretation of language will be like an act of violence as we wrest new meanings from what has been said. It is interesting to notice that not only theologians but psychiatrists and educators have also drawn on the resources of Heidegger's philosophy, though, again, he never in his life dealt explicitly with the problems of psychiatry or education. Although Heidegger never wrote any book on the subject of religion, and although he was reticent on the themes of God and theology, there are many brief allusions to those themes throughout his works. Many of these allusions are obscure. They are not all easily harmonized. And yet there is more than enough to show us a man deeply interested in theological questions, even if he did not think that a philosopher ought to involve himself directly.

When Heidegger died, the philosopher Hans Georg Gadamer was invited to give the memorial lecture, and he entitled it "An Invocation to the Vanished God." He declared in that lecture: "It was Christianity that provoked and kept alive this man's thought. It was the ancient transcendence and not modern secularity that spoke through him." And surely it was no accident that the words "Only a God Can Save Us" were chosen as the title for an article in the magazine *Der Spiegel*. That article consisted of an interview that Heidegger had given some time before his death on the condition that it would not be published until he had died.

Near the beginning of Heidegger's major work *Being and Time*, there is a brief mention of theology, which goes as follows:

> Theology is seeking a more primordial interpretation of man's being toward God, prescribed by the meaning of faith itself, and remaining within it. It is slowly beginning to understand once more Luther's insight, that the foundation on which its system of dogma rests has not arisen from an investigation in which faith was primary, and

that conceptually this foundation is not only inadequate for the problematic of theology, but conceals and distorts it.[3]

These are just a couple of sentences, but, as you can see, there is a lot packed into them. The remark occurs in a passage in which Heidegger is discussing what constitutes progress in any science. He holds that it is not the accumulation of information, not the discovery of new facts that counts as progress, but rather the capacity of a science to undergo a revolution in its basic concepts, to achieve a whole new way of understanding its subject matter. He then went on to give examples of fundamental changes that were taking place at that time (he was writing in 1927) in mathematics, physics, biology, the historical sciences, and, finally, theology.

Heidegger was at that time teaching in the University of Marburg, and one of his colleagues was a theologian, Rudolf Bultmann. It is not, I think, therefore difficult to identify the profound theological changes to which Heidegger was referring in the two sentences that I quoted. Barth, Gogarten, Bultmann, and other theologians of what was then the younger generation were asserting the independence of their subject, the autonomy of theology as over against philosophy. They were trying to find the foundations within faith itself, and, in particular, they were discarding the old natural theology and the metaphysics that went along with it, in the belief that these were damaging to the true work of the theologian.

That this is the correct interpretation of Heidegger's comment on theology can now be confirmed by a lecture on theology that he had given in 1927. But because of his reticence on the subject and his unwillingness to take up any position, that lecture lay unpublished for more than forty years and has only become available relatively recently.[4] The lecture is very revealing, and it keeps philosophy and theology as far apart from each other as one could imagine. Philosophy, Heidegger tells us, has to do with the question of being. But theology is a special or a positive science and deals, not with being in general, but with one particular area of beings. To quote, "Theology is a positive science, and as such, absolutely different from philosophy."

A positive science, in Heidegger's terminology (he also calls them ontic sciences), deals with a particular region of objects or beings. On the other hand, philosophy, which he understands as ontology or the science of being, demands, he says, a fundamental shift of view. It involves shifting our sights from the things that are, or from any particular region of these, to the question of being itself. Thus, he went on to say, theology as a positive science is closer to chemistry and mathematics than it is to philosophy. Theology's closest neighbor, Heidegger suggests, is history. Theology as a science of faith, that is to say, of an intrinsically historical mode of being, is to the very core a historical science. So he was asserting in 1927.

There are a few other mentions of theology in *Being and Time*, and these vary between hostility and friendliness. Thus, while Heidegger in the passage already quoted seemed to be giving his approval to the efforts of theology to reconstruct itself on a foundation drawn from faith itself, we find him equally concerned that philosophy should purge itself of theological influences. He speaks of residues of Christian theology that have not as yet been radically extruded from philosophy.[5] And he obviously thinks that they should be. An example of such a residue is the belief that there are such things as eternal truths. That concept conflicts with Heidegger's own understanding of truth as an event—the event of uncovering, which is not something eternal or timeless but something that happens from time to time in human experience.

On the other side, we find him acknowledging that certain ideas that are important, both for his own philosophy and for the philosophy of other thinkers with whom he has some sympathy, have their origins in Christian theology. In particular, he observes that transcendence, understood in the sense of man's reaching beyond himself, has its roots in theology.[6] He also declares it to be no accident that the phenomenon of anxiety, so important for his own philosophy, has been studied chiefly in Christian theology.[7] The ambivalent attitude to theology and the insistence on the separation of philosophy and theology, continues in Heidegger's next major work, *The Introduction to Metaphysics*. That work opens with Leibniz's famous question, "Why are there beings rather than nothing?" According to Heidegger, that is the basic question for philosophy, but he says it is not really a question for theology, for the Christian believer thinks he already knows the answer. The answer he would give, according to Heidegger, is: "Everything that is, except God Himself, has been created by God. God Himself, the Uncreated Creator, is."[8]

Heidegger thinks that such an answer misses the point of the question "Why are there beings rather than nothing?" That question has to be understood at a deeper philosophical level. The question is properly an ontological question, which asks about the relation of beings to being, the relation of what is to the principle of being. The Christian doctrine of creation has misunderstood the question as an ontical one and traces back everything that is, except God, to something else that is, namely, God. This doctrine accounts for the existence of the beings in terms of another being, but it never really gets to the question of being itself. That is what Heidegger calls "onto-theology." Its error is to confuse beings with being. It accounts, as I say, for the existence of the beings in terms of another being. It assimilates being to the beings, for, says Heidegger, we think of being rigorously only when we think of it in its difference with beings, and of beings in their difference with being.[9] As he had already maintained in his inaugural lecture at Freiburg, one must think of being as wholly other than beings. Indeed, from the point of view of the sciences, which concern themselves with what is and nothing else, being must be counted as nothing. It is the nothing else with which science does not concern itself, for it is not anything that is. Heidegger, of course, was to some extent pulling the legs of his colleagues at that time because he asked: "What is philosophy about? The physicist studies matter and energy. The biologist studies living organisms. The historian studies history. What's left for the philosopher?" And Heidegger replied, "Nothing. But that's precisely what philosophy is about—the nothing, which is wholly other to the things that are."[10]

Although Heidegger was critical of theology as onto-theology, as an ontic science that can only confuse the issue if it is allowed to masquerade as philosophy or to influence philosophical inquiry, he immediately goes on in that same passage to offer some defense of theology within its own field as an exposition of faith. He states: "There is a thinking and a questioning elaboration of the world of Christian experience, that is to say, of faith. That is theology. Only epochs which no longer fully believe in the true greatness of the task of theology arrive at the disastrous notion that a philosophy can help to provide a refurbished theology, if not a substitute for theology, which will satisfy the needs and tastes of the time. For the original Christian faith, philosophy is foolishness."[11]

So you see, on the one hand, Heidegger seems to be saying—much as Hegel had done before him—that theology is inferior to philosophy. Theology speaks out of faith. It cannot ask the radical philosophical question of being. It cannot bring all these ideas into a conceptual framework. Theology has not achieved conceptual clarity, and, in particular, it has remained on the ontic level so that, as he says, it is more akin to chemistry or history than to philosophy. I hope the chemists and historians will pardon Heidegger's remark there, which I think is meant to be rather contemptuous. Yet, Heidegger, as we have seen, acknowledges that from the theological point of view philosophy may appear to be foolishness. Perhaps this opinion is formed because the conceptual nature of philosophy cannot adequately express the concreteness of faith. So we find him saying in another place: "*Causa sui*—to be the cause of itself—is the right name for the God of Philosophy. But man can neither pray nor sacrifice to this god. Before the *causa sui*, man can neither fall to his knees in awe, nor can he play music and dance before this god. The godless thinking, which must abandon the God of Philosophy, god as *causa sui* is thus perhaps closer to the Divine God."[12]

I think when Heidegger wrote these words he surely had in

mind Pascal's famous contrast between the God of Philosophy, this abstract, bloodless construct of the intellect, and the God of Abraham, Isaac, and Jacob. But I think we have to ask, Has all theology been onto-theology? Have Christian thinkers always considered God as another being in addition to the beings in the world, as something else that is beyond whatever is within the world? Is God another being of the same order, shall we say, as the beings in the world? Or has the very use of an expression like *ens causa sui* indicated a reality that cannot really belong within the realm of the ontic, though indeed no language seems to be available to speak of it?

Admittedly, Christian theology has been confused on the point, and its language has been inadequately analyzed. But the mystical tradition in particular has been aware of the difference between God and the beings. Although our language objectifies God, the reality of God lies beyond the objectification. In one of his works, Heidegger reports a conversation that he had had with a Japanese philosopher, who said to him at one point: "For us, 'the void' is the highest name for what you like to express by the word 'being.'"[13] There's a strange ambivalence that, in one philosophy, what appears as 'being,' in another appears as 'the void,' as nothing. Admittedly, this remark was made by the Japanese man from the standpoint of Buddhism, but Christian mystics, too, notably John Eckhart, whose thought has many similarities to Heidegger, could have said much the same. And he was aware that God is not to be found in the realm of what is, so that, in one sense, he is nothing that is.

But it is not only in explicitly mystical writers but in a much broader stream of Christian theology that there struggles to find expression the difference between God and the objects that exist in the world, a difference resembling that which Heidegger finds between being and the beings. In recent theology, Paul Tillich, for instance, has brought clearly to expression the understanding of God as being. We must therefore be careful not to allow Heidegger to decide what theologians are permitted to say, and this means we cannot accept that all theology is onto-theology, or that it is merely ontic science, if indeed I may follow Heidegger in speaking of a "merely" ontic science.

Let us consider for a moment the classical theism of Saint Thomas. It is true that in the five ways of proving that there is a God, Thomas uses descriptions that seem to suggest a being, something that is, even if it is in a highly distinctive way. And yet, if one considers what must be involved in notions like "first cause," "prime mover," "necessary being," and so on, one sees that these cannot be additional items of the same order. A first cause must be different altogether from all subsequent causes. Rather, these phrases try to speak of the very ground of all the other items embraced in the order. It is not an attempt to explain some entities in terms of another entity, and it is not what Heidegger thought it was, an attempt to explain the beings in terms of another being. It is rather an attempt to indicate, however, inadequately, the ground of all entities or beings. This is true, even if the attempt is not particularly successful or if it is confused.

When Thomas says that "*qui est*," or "he who is," is the most appropriate name of God, this might seem again to be a clear proof that he thinks of God as a being, of an entity among others. And yet he explicitly says that this name is appropriate because it does not signify any particular form, but rather existence itself—*ipsum esse*. God is, therefore, being itself. Thomas explains, and I quote, that "since the existence of God is his essence, and since this is true of nothing else, it is clear that this name is especially appropriate to God, for the meaning of a name is the form of the thing named." We ought to notice, however, that whereas Thomas holds that it is true only of God that his essence is his existence, Heidegger claims that this is also the case with human beings.

Let us ask, then, is there anything in Heidegger's philosophy that might properly be called God, even if he himself does not use that expression? According to one of those who has written on Heidegger, Karl Löwith, his philosophy is, in its very essence, a theology without God. But that may be too hasty a judgment, and in any case, what does a theology without God mean? To try to pursue this question further, let us look in more detail at the notion of being in Heidegger. It is, of course, the question of being that was central throughout most of his philosophical career. That is the question that is taken up in his major early work *Being and Time*. That was not, as was sometimes supposed, a book discussing the nature of the human being. It was not even a book of metaphysics, though it still does not show Heidegger's later objection to metaphysics. His rejection, or, better, his overcoming of metaphysics, finds clear expression in the introduction that he provided for his lecture "What Is Metaphysics?" Heidegger recalls the works of Descartes in which he compared the whole of philosophy with a tree of which the roots are metaphysics; the trunk, physics; and the branches that come out of the trunk, the other sciences. But, Heidegger says, you have to go beyond that picture. Descartes described the tree, and he even got as far as the roots, but we are asking, "What is the ground in which the roots of the tree of philosophy have taken hold?" The trouble with metaphysics, Heidegger believes, is the same as the trouble with theology. Metaphysics concentrates its attention on what there is, on the beings as beings. It belongs to onto-theology. It stops short of the more fundamental task of inquiring into being, which, as he had pointed out in his lecture "What Is Metaphysics?," is taken to be nothing by those who are concerned with whatever is and nothing else.

In the introduction to that lecture, Heidegger speaks of being in a way that suggests that if being is not the same as God, at least it seems to be furnished with attributes and properties that could well be called divine or holy. It is not surprising that in a postscript to the lecture, he claims that the confrontation with this mysterious other, which is both nothing and being, awakens an anxiety that is very close to awe.

It is in his *Letter on Humanism*, however, that Heidegger uses the most exalted language about being and its relation to human beings. There we find him saying, "Before he speaks, man must let himself be addressed by being."[14] Admittedly, in that *Letter on Humanism*, he says explicitly in one place that being is not God. But in the very next sentence, he makes it clear that by "God" he understands a being in the onto-theological or metaphysical sense. On the other hand, he explicitly dissociates himself from Sartre's atheism. Sartre had quoted a sentence from *Being and Time* to the effect that only as long as a human understanding of being is possible is there being, suggesting that being is nothing but a concept in the human mind. Sartre took this to mean that man himself is the ultimate, and that being is a product of his subjectivity. But Heidegger says here that this is a misrepresentation of his thought. In the German, the expression "there is being" appears as "es gibt Sein." And Heidegger claims that these words "es gibt Sein" are not to be taken in the weak sense of "there is" or "there is being" but quite literally as "it gives being." And if one asks, "What gives?," then the answer, according to Heidegger, is that being gives and communicates itself to human beings. Thus, in contrast to Sartre's existentialism, which is also an atheistic humanism, Heidegger is able to declare, "Man is not the lord of the beings; man is the shepherd of being."[15] Yet we also encounter in this letter Heidegger's typical reluctance to speak of God. Although he dissociates himself from atheism, nothing is decided about God. He says being is not the same as God. One would have to move beyond the traditional metaphysical question about God's existence or nonexistence. Heidegger states: "Only from the truth of being can the essence of the holy be thought. Only from the essence of the holy is the essence of divinity to be thought. Only in the light of the essence of divinity can it be thought or said what the word 'God' is to signify."[16]

Is there any understanding of God, then, lying behind these remarks of Heidegger? It is clear, I think, that he is not a theist in the traditional metaphysical sense. But it is equally clear that he is not an atheist, if that term is taken in its broad sense to mean one who denies the holiness of being. I would agree with a Canadian philosopher who has recently been writing on this subject, John R. Williams, who says that Heidegger's thought could well be described as a pan-entheism,[17] and that it is an expression that has been used also to speak of the philosophy of, say, Whitehead. It is an understanding of God in which God is not entirely separate from the world, but the world is, shall we say, included within God. It is very important, of course, to notice that he says pan-entheism, not pantheism, which is something entirely different and is the identification of God with the physical universe.

This label, pan-entheism, is perhaps not in itself important, but it does place Heidegger in the succession of mystics like John Eckhart, who spoke of a God beyond God, so to speak, a Godhood that cannot be contained within the traditional concept of God. It aligns him also with a whole tradition in which I think one would include Hegel and Whitehead and quite a number of modern theologians. This relation to the mystical tradition is confirmed when we take into account Heidegger's doctrine of thinking. In his later work, he rarely uses the word "philosophy" at all. He prefers to speak of "thinking." He takes over a term from the mystic Eckhart. The word in German is *Gelassenheit*, and it means something like serenity, nonattachment, collectedness. It is attained by meditation—a kind of thinking that is open and receptive. Such thinking, according to Heidegger, is the proper concern of the philosopher. Indeed, he calls himself more and more a thinker and less and less a philosopher. This meditative thinking is close to the reflection of the poet. On the other hand, it contrasts with the active, calculative thinking of science and technology. And also, Heidegger contrasts it with the assured faith of theology. Whether he does justice to either science or theology is, of course, in question, but we need not pause to look into it at this time.

The thinking of which Heidegger speaks is a thinking that waits, and this idea of waiting introduces another important aspect in what he has to say about God or the divine. At the beginning of *Being and Time*, he says that time is the possible horizon for any understanding whatsoever of being.[18] Heidegger's being is not static. It includes becoming. It has a history. In the West, from the time of the Greek philosophers onward, there was been a forgetting of being. There has been a preoccupation with the beings. We have been more and more preoccupied with the objects within the world, but we have given up asking these questions: "Why are there such objects at all? What is the meaning of the being that manifests itself in these objects?"

Heidegger declares, "In the beginning of Western thinking, being is thought, but not the 'it gives' as such. The latter withdraws in favor of the gift which it gives." But it seems doubtful that this forgetting is culpable. Perhaps it comes about through the withdrawing of the being's self-communication. I quote Heidegger again: "What is history-like in the history of being is obviously determined by the way in which being takes place, and by this alone. This means the way in which it gives being. The forgetting of being, the preoccupation with the beings, leads eventually to the age of technology, of subjectivism, and of the will to power."

Heidegger, as is well known, was a great admirer of the poetry of Hölderlin, who in the nineteenth century was giving expression to the new sense of alienation that was making itself felt at that time. But Hölderlin's language was religious. According to him, the Gods have departed from the earth. They have not ceased to exist, but they are absent. They do not communicate themselves any more. Still, the very perception of the absence of the Gods is an acknowledgment of them. But, says Heidegger, whether God lives or remains dead is not determined by the religiousness of man, and still less by the theological aspirations of philosophy and of science. Whether God is God is determined from and within the constellation of being.[19] Here I would like to allude again to that article entitled "Only a God Can Save Us," which appeared at the time of Heidegger's death. In this article, Heidegger was asked by one of his interviewers if he was a pessimist. He replied that he was neither a pessimist nor an optimist. Even the experience of the absence of God is a liberation from complete fallenness into the beings. But, he says, we cannot think God into being. We can only make a preparation, either for his appearing or for his absence.

As he was also fond of saying, we live between the times.

The Gods of the past have faded away, and the God who is to come has not yet arrived. As Hölderling expressed it in one of his poems, "The Father has averted his face." We are waiting and hoping for a new advent.

Mentioning this dynamic and even apocalyptic element in Heidegger's thinking about God and being directs our attention to still another concept that appears only in his late writings— *Das Ereignis,* meaning "The Event." John R. Williams believes that finally it is The Event rather than being that most closely corresponds to God in Heidegger's philosophy. What is The Event? It seems to be the 'It gives' that we have met already, the "it gives" whereby being communicates with man and in a sense entrusts itself to humanity. We read in one section in Heidegger's writing: "There is nothing else to which one could trace back the event, or in terms of which it could be explained. The event is not the result of something else, but an act of giving that reaches out and imparts like an 'it gives' something which even being needs to attain its own character as presence."

These sentences, which are admittedly obscure, would seem to support Williams' contention that The Event is the ultimate concept in Heidegger's philosophy. But I myself would be reluctant to follow Williams when he says that The Event is beyond being. I find it difficult to attach meaning to the expression "beyond being," and especially so in a discussion of Heidegger, whose concept of "being" never means the sum of the beings, the totality of what is, but has already been declared to be totally other than everything that is. I would think of The Event as an event within being, or perhaps, if you like, it is the event of being, the event that indeed constitutes being and reveals the essence of being. If that event is the "it gives," and this is, so to speak, the heart of being, then it is surely close to what the religious believer names as God. For is not God the Self-Giver, the one whose overflowing generosity shares the gift of being with another to whom he may be present? Is there not, in other words, a God of love at the end of those paths of thinking along which Heidegger invites us to walk?

Let me come back to Gadamer's memorial lecture. He says—I think, rightly—that those who have studied Heidegger will never again read the words "being," "spirit," "God" in the way they were understood in traditional metaphysics. But then he asks why someone who found theological questions so fascinating was not himself a theologian and why he stood off from theology. Because, replies Gadimer, he was a thinker. It was thinking that was at work in him. He felt no empowerment to speak of God. But what would be needed to speak of God, and that it would not do to speak of him as the scientists speak of their projects—that was the question that stirred him and showed him the path of thinking.

NOTES

1. *Unterwegs zur Sprache* (Pfullingen, 1965), p. 96.
2. *Identity and Difference* (New York, 1969), p. 55.
3. *Being and Time* (New York, 1962), p. 30.
4. See *The Piety of Thinking* (Bloomington, 1976), p. 6.
5. *Being and Time*, p. 272.
6. *Ibid.*, p. 74.
7. *Ibid.*, p. 492, n. iv.
8. *Introduction to Metaphysics* (New Haven, 1959), p. 7.
9. *Identity and Difference*, p. 62.
10. See *Was Ist Metaphysik?* (Frankfurt, 1949), pp. 26–7.
11. *Introduction to Metaphysics*, p. 7.
12. *Identity and Difference*, p. 72.
13. *Unterwegs zur Sprache*, p. 109.
14. *Über den Humanismus* (Frankfurt, 1947), p. 10.
15. *Ibid.*, p. 29.
16. *Ibid.*, pp. 36–7.
17. See *Martin Heidegger's Philosophy of Religion* (Waterloo, 1977), p. 154.
18. *Being and Time*, p. 19.
19. *Die Technik und die Kehre* (Pfullingen, 1962), p. 46.

The Reality of God and the Future of the Human Project

DAVID JENKINS

IT IS COMMONPLACE that we are now one world, and as such a limited world and a threatened world. It is commonplace, but the knowledge, the reflection and the inescapable assumption of being one world are given no common place in practice in the actual pursuit of politics or industry and commerce or religion. Everyone gets on with doing their own thing, in religion as much as anything else. Further, in religion they do this with a singular additional paradoxical twist because in most current and developed religions the alleged object or subject of the religious quest, practice and claim is, in some sense or other, claimed to be the one true God of the whole earth and, indeed, of the whole universe—or the fundamental spiritual principle and insight thereof.

I have therefore taken the honour and opportunity of your invitation to me to give a lecture under the auspices of the Chair of Judeo-Christian studies here in Tulane University to offer the absurdly wide and possibly pretentious title of "The Reality of God and the Future of the Human Project." I have done this in order to focus on one particular question which is now posed with especial sharpness and urgency to all Jews, Christians and Muslims. It is a question which has been around at least potentially since the time of Moses and has emerged in various actual and historical forms with the split between Jews and Christians and then with the life of Muhammad and the rise of Islam. However, as I shall try to show, it is singularly pressing now and can be argued to be a question which is urgent not only for the adherents of Judaism, Christianity and Islam but also for the whole human race. The question is: "Can a faith in the one true God which arises out of the tradition of monotheism arrived at in the Jewish scriptures and/or in those scriptures with the Christian scriptures added to them be anything but exclusivist and therefore necessarily in conflict with any other tradition of monotheism so arising?"

To put the issue more bluntly and directly: is it the inevitable logic of Christian faith that Christians must expect, in the name and power of God, to convert all Jews and Muslims? Is it in the inevitable logic of Jewish belief in God that Jews must survive *exclusively* as Jews until God mops up the Christians, the Muslims and the rest? Is it the inevitable logic of commitment to Allah through the Quranic revelation and obedience dictated to Muhammad that the Muslims must be ready for *Jihad* until Islam is victorious against all enemies and unbelievers? And does this inevitability arise because of the very sense of calling by, encounter with and revelation from the one true God which constitutes the defining characteristic of the various faiths?

If so, the outlook for the world and the human project within it is poor, for the world needs some powerful and yet open form of human unity. Also, the outlook for convinced and convincing belief in one true God who truly exists and truly is God is also poor. For his professed and devoted adherents contradict one another and, in actual history, sometimes destroy one another. At this juncture in our human affairs, therefore, does God have any relevance to the human future and, if so, what is that relevance? You could, of course, turn that question inside out and ask: "Given the history of the monotheistic faiths derived from the influence of the biblical tradition and given the pressures that are now upon us in our one and limited world, would we not be best advised to work and to do the equivalent of pray for the establishment of a realistic and open atheism?" The question in that case would then be: "And where shall we find ourselves if we succeed in doing that?"

Clearly, the reality of the situation with regard to the existence, nature and activity of God is exceedingly unclear, not least because of the behaviour, claims and history of his self-styled faithful, whatever their tradition or form of commitment—or rather I should say, whatever our tradition of faith and commitment. For I am myself a convinced and committed Christian who has a strong and increasing sense of calling to the job I am at present doing and to the representative role I am at present occupying.

Those of us who are caught up into the practice and pursuit of a faith are therefore confronted with the actual practical effects of people holding and expressing what they believe and claim to be "true faith." This is a very ambiguous term. Presumably it takes its legitimizing role among religious people from its implication or claim that the faith being held, celebrated, expressed and lived out is an authentic and appropriate response to the way things are and will be and, in particular, to the being, nature and purposes of God in his relation to the totality of things. In practice, however, to show "true faith" seems to be a matter of commitment, of readiness to make demands and readiness to take urgent action of some sort, independently of the truth, coherence or appropriateness of the religious story, theory or system which forms the background to, and the basis of, the religious tradition within which the "true faith" is being expressed. Religious renewal or revival seem most frequently to be associated with heightened fervour, increased demands and readiness for distinctive and decisive actions, and strengthened dogmatism or even fundamentalism. All this gives increased coherence to the group involved but accentuates their exclusion of, and difference from, their neighbours in general or from their co-religionists in particular.

Of course, if religious faith kindles no fervour and makes no difference then there would seem to be little point or power in it. At the heart of any tradition of religious faith is the conviction or hope of what might be called a saving impact. God is the saving resource and promise. Being saved involves being saved from something and being saved for something, and that must involve producing a difference and making a change.

Hence, in principle, we should expect people who are caught up in a "true faith" to be different, to be changed and then to be agents of change. But when we see how religious devotees and enthusiasts are in fact different, and what they are changed into and what changes they seek to bring about, we may well be inclined to come to the conclusion that if religious faith reflects something to do with salvation or with being on the way to salvation, then whatever the salvation saves from the cure is worse than the disease. Indeed, there are good grounds, both in history and in contemporary experience, for regarding religion as part of the pathological and diseased side of human life.

Yet we who are caught up by and into a religious faith or, as we might dare to say and feel compelled to say, caught up by and into God, cannot accept this diagnosis. How then shall we face this challenge? I suggest we might find a way forward by pursing the question "Does God have favourites?" If we find that our tradition of faith and our practice of faith obliges us to answer this question "Yes, God does seem to have favourites," then it would be necessary to press the question "And what does God have favourites for?" This question, I believe, would bring us back to my topic, namely: "The Reality of God and the Future of the Human Project."

I will therefore pursue my Christian self-questioning thus. The issue of the reality of God may, on reflection, and on reflection on the behaviour and claims of the various faithful worshippers of God, appear to be very uncertain and possibly unhelpful or even harmful. The reality and problem of our *one world*, however, is both clearer and more plainly and evidently universal in scope than any religious tradition or self-styled faith.

We all know now that we live on a small and limited planet which we are both overcrowding and overusing. The picture of the earth relayed back to us from space provides the unforgettable concrete image and symbol of this. The world is now one financial system, and the system is highly volatile and fragile. It is overburdened with debt. In your rich country you have the double deficit of both budget and trade. Among the poor countries of the Third World there are those which are getting more into debt in order to finance the interest on the debt they already have. Moreover the system is now linked up on computers in such a way that it is programmed to respond to its own responses. This is clearly a structure made for turbulence and collapse.

Moreover what keeps it going is growth in both production and consumption. But this sort of growth has already produced ecological erosion of very threatening extent. We can now all know clearly that we are steadily using up the non-renewable resources and even the very substance of our strictly limited and heavily populated planet, at rates which are debatable with regard to each particular resource but in an overall way which is undeniable. Forests are being felled without restraint, despite repeated warnings, and this not only destroys the possibility of a steady growth of further trees but encourages atmospheric changes which lead to deserts, which are also encouraged by the erosion of soil when the trees have gone. The ozone layer which helps make sunlight healthy and life-giving when it reaches us is under threat from our pollution and is as good as pierced already in some recognizable spots. The disappearance of living species proceeds apace and the encouraging and multiplying efforts of conservation are, nonetheless, at the same time further symptoms of how we are turning the world into a desert. Even our love for the countryside threatens it, as the recreational invasion of our wilderness makes increasingly clear. So our method of keeping our finances and economics going threatens the very ability of our world to sustain itself and support us.

It also threatens any sort of viable and sustainable community in the world. This is vividly illustrated for me by what I have come to call the barbed-wire divide. This symbol came into my head and has stayed hauntingly with me ever since I happened to see a short sequence on television news which showed Archbishop Runcie visiting Soweto with Archbishop Tutu. One sequence was filmed, so to speak, from outside in, and running across the centre of the screen was a barbed-wire entanglement: to mark, as it seemed to me, the need to defend white prosperity from black poverty. About the same time I also saw a brief moment of a film about the United States border with Mexico and the need for ceaseless vigilance and pretty violent measures to protect that border against the steady flow of poor people from the South pressing into your dreamt-of Eldorado—and incidentally running, some of them, drugs and committing other illegalities. The film implied that nothing would actually keep the tide back. Again I had the sense of the have-nots pressing desperately, although as yet not with any organized violence, into the land of the haves—where they would, of course, find many fellow have-nots. For the "barbed-wire divide" is also symbolic of increasing divisions, certainly in both the United States and in Britain and, I believe, in other Western countries. There is a clear, and worsening, division between those who are in the system and can increasingly purchase its benefits, and those who are out of the system who can never get the chance of either forming a market or joining in a market. Will it be necessary to hive them all off into ghettos, surrounded by barbed wire and patrolled, I suppose, by increasing numbers of police and soldiers? So we have "Third Worlds" (as you might say) both within us and all around us.

On top of this it seems almost too much to add to the apocalyptic pressures by bringing in the threats of nuclear war and the uncertainties of nuclear power, but they must clearly never be forgotten. It may be that these threats are at last being seriously reduced, and it may be that nuclear power can be handled in sufficiently positive and safe ways, but to do either of these things successfully requires great trust, great patience and great collaboration. Shall we get this in a world made so unstable and uncertain by global financial instability, by ecological erosion and by the barbed-wire divide? The pressures upon us all in our one world to recognize our unity within the limits of our globe and to work together to discover new ways of organizing our lives and systems so that Third World countries can develop an economic independence within which they can work out their own sustainable ways of flourishing and so that First and Second World countries can settle down to ways of life which are saved from excessive consumption and thus sustainable, renewable and shareable, are clear, urgent and ought to be irresistible.

But the human race as organized into states and nations seems to have no more practical sense of what is required of it, and offered to it by way of global survival and sustainable and shareable life, than religious people who are organized into various traditions, communities and churches seem to have of the practical and spiritual implications of the transcendent oneness and mystery of God, if he exists and is indeed God. Might it be possible, therefore, that the ignored threats to our one world and the apparently self-contradictory practices of our "true" faiths could interact in a positive, creative and future-enhancing way?

From within one of the faiths which have grown out of the biblical tradition this is not only a proper, but also a necessary, question to ask. First, it is of the very essence of a religious faith to be a "true faith." As Kenneth Cragg puts it in a magnificently stimulating book: "It is not in the nature of religion to consent to be indifferent about its own claims."[1] To be caught up in faith in God within any religious tradition, community, story and framework is to be caught up in offers of finality, demands of totality, experiences of utter but gracious dependence and promises of over-riding and invincible joy and love. There can be no half-measures about the offers, demands and implications of God. There can be, and there of course is, a sad and nearly infinite variety of half-measures, no measures and inappropriate measures by which the would-be or self-styled "faithful" respond, or fail to respond, to God. Everybody sins, and religious people sin religiously. This very obvious and deeply troubling fact can be transposed, from the perspective and problematic of this particular enquiry, into the statement that all we faithful sin faithlessly: both as individuals and in our various groupings, communities and institutions. The question is whether this practical and long-continued contradiction decisively destroys any claims to reality or truth conveyed in, or pointed to by, the "true religion" of whatever tradition. Or are the human contradictions of the faithful religious in the practice of their religion one pointed, distressing and diagnostic case of that whole range of human contradictions of, and fighting against, the true, the good, the hopeful, the beautiful and the loving which make us, despite our being so great a resource for love, discovery and progress, yet our own worst enemies? This is a fundamental religious and human question, a question about the ultimate nature of things and about what resources there are available to us for life and human living in, through and beyond the universe. It is, in fact, the question of God to which all "true faiths" are a joyously positive and potentially all-demanding and all-embracing response. Therefore, faithful believers (and every appropriate institution within the tradition of each one's faith) are bound to respond to the contradictions of their faith from within the resources of their faith, however far outside the presently understood boundaries of that faith such a contradiction and challenge may take them or us when properly, hopefully and graciously faced.

So a contradiction to a true faith—or to the very idea of there validly being such a thing as a true faith—has to be faced, by believers, from within the resources and truth of their faith. After all, for a believer, a faithful and faith-seeking believer, there is nowhere else to turn—and nowhere else to which he or she should, would or could turn. But there is a further point from within the particular tradition and faith in which I myself am caught up and to which I remain wholeheartedly committed by renewed and reflective choice, as well as, I believe, by divine graciousness, which is an infinitely greater and more necessary cause than my own weak will and limited intellect. This arises from what I will call the prophetic insight and tendency to discern if not the hand of God, then the touch and the invitation of God, in certain convergences of events and experiences which call our humanity, our faith, our religion and our world in question. Judgment to condemnation is opportunity for renewal. Death is the way to life. The undermining of the old and the oppressive is a breaking out into newness and liberation: if faith can discern, obedience can respond and grace be received. Thus the coming together of a recognition of the failure of the witness of our respective "true faiths" to the glory, reality, demands and offers of the one true God with a recognition of the urgent threats to our one world would seem a wholly appropriate pressure, provocation and promise for prophetic discernment and for religious repentance, obedience and renewal. Might this not be the proper and urgent way forward for the sake of him who is the worship of all our faiths and in the service of the world which is his and of all humanity who are his?

As I wrote this, and as I say this under the specific auspices of a Chair of Judeo-Christian Studies, I could not and cannot but be aware of a very particular calling in question which we who are Jews and we who are Christians must be confronting as we seek for effective renewal of faith, prophecy and action at this very moment in this very world. This is the reality of Auschwitz and the reality of anti-semitism to which Christianity has made such a major contribution. I have no time here to refer to the great amount of most important and challenging material which has been produced and is being produced around this theme, save to say that any following up of the agenda which is being pointed to in my lecture will require the most serious study and digestion of this material. For now, I make just one point, as follows.

Both Jews and Christians exercised the sort of prophetic discernment I am talking about on the fall of Jerusalem in AD 70. This is well put in an early chapter of *Approaches to Auschwitz: The Legacy of the Holocaust:*

> Both the Jews and the Christians were nurtured spiritually by scripture to believe that God is the sovereign lord of history who controls the destiny of all nations. Both believed that God had entered into a covenant with the chosen people and that Israel's ruin was explained by both as due to a failure to keep the covenant and God's inevitable response. Where they differed was in the view they each held of the sin by which Israel had been chastized . . . the Christians

believed that Jerusalem fell because the Jews had rejected Jesus Christ. For the rabbis Jerusalem fell because the nation failed to obey God's commandments as they were interpreted by the Pharisees.[2]

This way of proceeding has been devastatingly called in question by what has actually happened. On the Jewish side it would seem just possible to contain the fall of Jerusalem within an understanding of the just judgment and the loving providence of God. Can this possibly be done with the Holocaust? On the Christian side it might have been just possible to contain a Christian understanding of God's temporary judgment on the Jews within a loving and obedient response to a merciful and gracious God if we had taken with absolute and consistent seriousness Paul's sure and certain vision in Romans 11 that, in God's mysterious purposes, Jews and Christians would ultimately share in one salvation and fulfilment and that this was necessarily so because of the very nature and being of God. But in practice the "prophetic" discernment turned into charges of deicide and justification for pogroms, persecutions and persistent practices which make such sickening reading that few of us Christians even know about them, let alone begin to face up to them. The stain and damage would seem well nigh ineradicable, even without its climax in contributing to making the Holocaust possible. Maybe we should say that in their use of prophetic discernment the Jews were sadly mistaken and the Christians more wickedly perverse, but in either case, or putting them both together, is not the whole procedure permanently discredited?

Perhaps then we should cede the living remnants of the biblical tradition of monotheism to the Muslims. At least they are clear that God must be visibly victorious. This is why Jesus is second to Muhammad as a prophet and servant of God. Muhammad succeeded, while Jesus failed. Because Jesus was indeed a prophet and servant of God, God did not allow death to seal Jesus' failure; rather, he was "raptured" away from that death—but the future of God's purposes lies with the followers of the Prophet. Yet here again all did not go as the first followers and readers of the Quran might have expected. In today's threatened and precarious world it is by no means clear that as the followers of the Prophet pursue their understanding of the purposes and calling of God for the world they will avoid precipitating the blowing up of that world.

Perhaps, therefore, we should cede the whole pursuit of spirituality in our crises of humanity and the world to the Hindus and the Buddhists. They have always known that the whole trouble is Illusion—about the reality of the world, about our separate selves, and about all the things that trouble and threaten us. If we are convinced that we must not do this because, despite all contradictions, threats and uncertainties, we are held by the richness of the world, the richness of persons, and the glories glimpsed through and beyond our traditions so that we must persist in praise, in suffering and in hope, then we must still clearly face the atheists. What can our struggling on be but self-deception, and what can our bursts of praise be but whistling in the dark? The whole notion of making ultimate sense, of there being a human project which comes from anywhere, or is going anywhere, and the whole notion of going beyond all projects and ultimate sense to Nirvana are all alike pieces of semantic nonsense. Why continue to play with them when we require all our spiritual, mental and physical capacities to preserve what world we have for what hope we can enjoy?

But supposing our faith, our spirituality, our community, our tradition, our worship and our experience, both individual and corporate, of what we must call God and which will not let us go, all insist that we should carry on: as Jews, as Christians, as Muslims and as Jews, Christians, Muslims of our particular and peculiarly devout sort? Shall we then fall back on sectarianism? God *has* his favourites, and they are to be found above all among ourselves, strengthened, defined, upheld and continued by what has been given us in our tradition, history and faith and in its special and particular peculiarity. It is this very favouritism which allows us to exist and to continue to exist. God calls us to be what we are and God sustains us by keeping us what we are. So, of course, out of the very essence and practice of our existence and calling we must exclude other claimants to favouritism, either as against us or at least as not of us. How else can we survive—or be true to that which has given us existence and enables us to survive? Whatever may be the practical and functional truth in this claim and experience of favouritism in relation to calling, encounter, inspiration and revelation, surely it must all be placed in a much wider context than where we "religiously," in all our traditions, hold and confine it, thereby distorting it. We must be challenged again and again—and more and more deeply, painfully and sharply about such "favouritism." Maybe it does reflect a real, vital and important way of God's working and of God's making himself known. But what is it actually for?

Can there be any creative and realistic way forward, given the needs of the world, given the flawed histories of all of us, given the reality of God which we all claim and acknowledge—and, as some sort of immediate prophetic and demanding symbol to us, given what is going on in and around Jerusalem and Israel at this very moment? For Jews and Christians Israel/Palestine is the holy land, Jerusalem is our holy city and in it are the holy places of Islam. Yet, at the moment Jerusalem and some of the parts of Palestine/Israel are, perhaps, one of the most unhappy and unhallowing areas in the world. I cannot even use geographical and state nomenclature without causing offence to some community or other and seeming to take sides in a bitter battle. Here hitherto oppressed Jews are behaving as oppressors or looking like oppressors, however much they are forced into this, or claim to be forced into this. Here Muslim sensibilities are being outraged, Palestinians are being killed and Arab inhabitants are being displaced and forced into being, or remaining, refugees. Here local Christians are among the Arabs and foreign resident Christians seem to be utterly confused and still, if reports are to be believed, to be keeping up their internal quarrels about who shall maintain which part of the Church of the Holy Sepulchre. Moreover the quarrels in, and the quarrels about, this holy land threaten to embroil great powers and the whole world and certainly have repercussions among the great powers and throughout the whole world. Are we to interpret this in a sectarian way as threatening (and as some fanatics believe, promising) Armageddon and the end of the world? Or are we to see it as an urgent divine demand and an immediate human plea to all of us, Jews, Christians and Muslims, to work out a speedy, practical and common repentance which is worthy of our deepest religious convictions and our truest knowledge of God? All the more so as our Mediterranean "holy land" is *not* the holy land of the East? Is our distracted and distorted "holiness" to be their and our destruction? Is that what he whom we all believe to be the God of the whole universe wants his quarreling and divided "favourites" to do for him and offer to him? Is this the meaning of our calling, our devotion, our worship and our hope?

I judged that I had to raise these questions and draw attention to this agenda because the threat to our one world is so urgent, because the need for a reconciling unity of faith, resource and vision is so apparent, and because I cannot myself escape glimpses of the glory of God, however much he seems to be hidden, contradicted and ignored in practice, and however ingloriously and even shamefully I and my fellow co-religionists seem to respond to him. As you would expect from what I have said previously I can respond to the judgment, the crisis and the opportunity we are all in only from within the resources of my own tradition.

A final brief word, therefore, formulating the dilemma and the opportunity as I see it around the name and tradition of Jesus, whose name and what it should be taken for is, of course, a matter of contention among us. I offer the formulation first and principally as a challenge to us Christians to take up the dialogue, the disturbing investigations and, then, the practical actions which the questioning agenda I have been outlining above would suggest. I also hope it might be able to be offered, in the second place, to those Jews and Muslims who also find themselves to be called in question in order to see whether they could propose a corresponding and resonant formula from within their own faiths, traditions and devotion so that, however tentatively, some of us might begin to take steps together in moving beyond our mutual exclusiveness and our mutual conflicts to a more appropriate worship of our one God and more creative service of our one threatened human race.

The formulation is this: from a Christian point of view the present tragedy of the world and the present call to biblical monotheists might thus be described. The Jews have failed to recognize Jesus as the Messiah, the Christians have failed to obey Jesus as the Messiah, and the Muslims have chosen a warrior prophet instead. What that means is that we have all got God, to a large extent, wrong and so we are in the gravest possible danger of being one of the destructive threats to the future of the human race rather than God's offer of service to and for the whole human race. God is not principally to be conceived of as a mighty warrior or a dominating potentate to be served with exclusiveness and on one set of demanding and enforceable terms which are known to us alone (whichever of his "favourites" we are). God is himself (or himself and herself and itself—for God is anonymous and beyond all naming) the presence, service and power who is love, persuasion, endurance, suffering and joy which cannot and will not be fulfilled until all is fully shareable and fully shared. Hence, eventually, our dialogue, repentance and moving into appropriate actions must not be only among Jews, Christians and Muslims but also reaching out to, and in human pursuit with, Hindus and Buddhists, atheists and agnostics—and all searching, suffering and hoping human beings. But "judgment must begin at the house of God" (1 Peter 4:17), so the first challenge is to us who believe we are, somehow or other, God's chosen favourites, chosen particularly for God's universal purpose. That is to say that the first challenge concerning the reality of God and the future of the human project is to us Jews, Christians and Muslims.

So I must leave you, as is so often the case with sermons, and I fear sometimes the case with lectures, at the precise point at which we all ought to begin. Perhaps, because we all agree in confessing that God is merciful and gracious, we should help one another to cast ourselves on that grace and mercy so that we can find out what God wants to make of us, instead of continuing to insist on what we want to make of God.

NOTES

1. Kenneth Cragg, *The Christ and the Faiths: Theology in Cross-Reference* (London: SPCK Press, 1988), p. 319.

2. Richard L. Rubenstein and John K. Roth, *Approaches to Auschwitz: The Legacy of the Holocaust* (Philadelphia and London: Westminster John Knox and SCM Press, 1987), p. 41.